FINE LINES OF WELLNESS, ONE STEP BEYOND RECOVERY

Recovery from the effects of Alcoholism

LOIS MARIE

BALBOA PRESS
A DIVISION OF HAY HOUSE

Copyright © 2015 Lois Marie.

All rights reserved. No part of this book may be used or reproduced by any means, graphic, electronic, or mechanical, including photocopying, recording, taping or by any information storage retrieval system without the written permission of the author except in the case of brief quotations embodied in critical articles and reviews.

Balboa Press books may be ordered through booksellers or by contacting:

Balboa Press
A Division of Hay House
1663 Liberty Drive
Bloomington, IN 47403
www.balboapress.com
1 (877) 407-4847

Because of the dynamic nature of the Internet, any web addresses or links contained in this book may have changed since publication and may no longer be valid. The views expressed in this work are solely those of the author and do not necessarily reflect the views of the publisher, and the publisher hereby disclaims any responsibility for them.

The author of this book does not dispense medical advice or prescribe the use of any technique as a form of treatment for physical, emotional, or medical problems without the advice of a physician, either directly or indirectly. The intent of the author is only to offer information of a general nature to help you in your quest for emotional and spiritual well-being. In the event you use any of the information in this book for yourself, which is your constitutional right, the author and the publisher assume no responsibility for your actions.

Any people depicted in stock imagery provided by Thinkstock are models, and such images are being used for illustrative purposes only.
Certain stock imagery © Thinkstock.

Print information available on the last page.

ISBN: 978-1-5043-4066-3 (sc)
ISBN: 978-1-5043-4067-0 (e)

Balboa Press rev. date: 12/11/2015

To: My Parents
for Being the Catalyst

To: My Children
for Being the Courage

To: My Higher Power
for Being the Will

To: The Twelve Steps
For Making it Happen

By: I AM
Lois Marie

Contents

This is the Very Beginning of Wellness............................ 1
Weapons or Tools.. 3
Care-Giving or Care-Taking 7
Self-Indulgence or Self Nurturing 9
Vulnerability or Neediness 19
Action or Reaction 23
Building Walls or Creating Boundaries 33
Obsession or Discipline 44
Survivor (Foregiveness) or Victim.................................... 53
Selfish or Selfhood 57
Loneliness or Aloneness... 63
Secrecy or Privacy 73
In The Stars? or In Me? 81
Anger or Resentment.. 86
Being in Control or Being All Together.......................... 90
Controlling My Life or Living My Life 104

Awareness or Denial 109
Expectation or Preparation 118
Addictions or Habits 127
Impulse or Intuition 139
Interest or Curiosity 149
Building a Relationship or Taking a Hostage 156
Sensuality or Sexuality 166
Being Childish or Loving the Child 178
The Twelve Steps 184

This is the Very Beginning of Wellness

Hi, my name is Lois and I am the adult child of an alcoholic. I grew up in a family filled with alcohol abuse and violence. I married young, at 18, to a man who was an alcoholic and violent when he was drinking. The marriage lasted 10 years. This is a familiar story for many thousands of us. I never drank or did drugs, but I sure could not get my life in order. Everything turned to dust, and I had no idea why. I was raising two girls, well, attempting to raise two girls, but frankly, not doing a very good job, and I had no idea why. I found myself asking why I had no idea. It was a viscous circle. You know, walking around in circles is a very dizzying experience!! I had lost my equilibrium, my self, my family, my connection to the Universe. Life is kind of like that, I find, we get ourselves into these terrible pickles and if we are really really lucky, we see the lifeline coming our way. And that's what happened.

My lifeline was a group of people called Adult Children of Alcoholics and for two years I worked their program.

At the beginning of this journey I heard the words "We never recover". At the time they were the most devastating words I had ever heard. All this hard work! All this pain! Someone in our Twelve Step Group began to chuckle. "Of course we never recover, but we do get better". For a long time I had no idea what that meant. As I started to go through the pain work and reach healthier parts of myself, I began to realize that recovery work is ongoing. Ongoing on a daily basis.

I began devising a plan for myself that I could use one day at a time. What I discovered was that almost everything I used or misused had a fine line between helping and hindering. That fine line could very easily be crossed, either way. It all depended on which buttons were pushed.

These fine lines began to add up to my recovery. I pass them on to you. I hope they are of service.

WEAPONS or TOOLS

When we grow up in a dysfunctional environment we learn how to use all sorts of tools for survival. We learn the "fight or flight" tool. We learn how to be peacemakers. We learn early that we can get attention by being "bad". We learn how to be daddy's little girl or mommy's little boy. We learn that if we have a temper tantrum we often will get our own way. We learn to people-please to keep the peace. We learn how to become invisible. We learn how to fix things up between members of our family. We learn how to be the Star. We learn all of these things and more at the feet of our primary caregivers. And we learn them because our primary caregivers never learned there was another way.

So, all this baggage gets passed down from generation to generation – this tool box that has become a weapon.

Now, here we are, wandering around as adults, tool box in hand, going forth into the world to make our mark, and finding that the tool box is full of grenades, instead of working tools, and everything we touch ends up blowing up in our faces. And the Shrapnel from the impact goes off in various directions leaving a fallout along our trail, which not only leaves us desperately injured, but the people around us as well. What a mess. And we don't know what to do about it.

The only thing we do know is that nothing has worked out the way we thought it would, that we hurt all the time, physically, spiritually and emotionally and that life is a drudge. We find ourselves saying stuff like "Is this it?" "Is this all?" "My God, what have I done?" "What have you done to me?" "I can't stand this anymore." "I've got to get out." "I've got to run." "I've got to hide." "I hurt". "I've got to get even."

It is truly a mess. Those of us who have done recovery work have all been there.

We have experienced these and other emotions, taken a look at the weapons going off around us, wondering where in the hell they came from, wondering what we could possibly do with them, reached some sort of bottom. We have found ourselves in bars, on street corners, in psychiatric wards, in bad marriages, in dead end jobs, unemployed, with dysfunctional children, in constant states of crises. The bombs keep going off around us. The guns in our hands keep shooting away and we don't know how to stop it.

We are not in charge.

We have become hardened, overbearing, weak, winy, manipulative, angry, addicted, desperate, frightened – the list goes on.

Somewhere along this line we reach a place where nothing is working. Our health has become precarious, our emotional well being has become unraveled, our spirituality has become depleted, our entire trilogy has become totally fragmented.

We are one big, blubbering mess.

We can carry on like this, thinking the whole world is out to get us, or we can reach a bottom where we desperately need help.

Once we reach that bottom we can continue on through our downward spiral, or we can reach out for help. It is up to us. Most of the tools we learned to use as children don't work anymore, but we don't know that. How can we know that?

Our denial system is so in place, our walls are so thick, that it is impossible to see the forest for the trees.

And this leads us to the incredible gift of Alcoholics Anonymous and its various branches. We can begin to part that veil of denial and start taking measured looks into our lives, one day at a time, and begin our own journey of awareness. And, wow, is it a wonderful journey!!

These tools don't need to be weapons, we can change that!! Finer minds than mine have said that Alcoholics Anonymous is the greatest organization of the twentieth century. I bet it continues to be number one in the twenty first, as well.

Imagine, coming out of our self-imposed state of purgatory, and knowing that for the rest of our natural lives, we do not have to dodge bullets, keep our heads down, drink, use, or act out. What an incredible gift!!

Oh, and aside from all these gifts that AA and its many branches give, is that they save our lives. I am so grateful!!

Throughout the course of working the 12 steps, I learned that, although I hardly ever drank (allergic to it!), I absolutely had the alcoholic personality.

Once that veil of denial was lifted, the fine lines of wellness began to appear. The rage in my belly began to subside, I began to feel parts of myself that I never remembered feeling before. Other people in the group were having the same experience. Many of us noticed how much healthier we were all beginning to look and feel.

So that's the background. I can only delineate the lines on a very personal level, share some of my experiences with you and honour you enough to know that you will delineate your own lines between weapons and tools so that you, too, can polish up your tool box and get on with your healthy life.

If you have stuck with me so far, over the next many pages we will discover and discuss some of the many fine lines.

God Bless......

CARE-GIVING or CARE-TAKING

If we care take we do so because we are looking outside of ourselves to feel secure, and we very quickly become victims. If we care-give we do so because it makes us happy to reach out to someone, and we very quickly become winners. The trick is to know when to draw the line.

As a child I got pretty good at picking up after other people's baggage. The only problem was I never knew when to stop. Picking up after someone else's emotional crisis is fraught with problems. When we continue to pick up someone else's pieces, we are seldom teaching them or ourselves what it means to be a responsible adult. We are too busy enabling.

Some of the care-giving events were a real pleasure, especially as I recognized that sick need for control. My daughters' weddings are a perfect example. Each daughter married a good man and each daughter wanted the perfect wedding – in her own style. I didn't have much money to offer for the events, but I helped them choose their dresses, watched each walk down the isle with their father, and cried a tear or two at their vows. Their weddings, although very different, were beautiful, and they were what they wanted, not what I thought they should be.

I also learned how to look after myself during these times. I learned when to be of help and when to back away. And I learned that when I needed rest, it was my responsibility to just take the time.

I also learned what I could and could not do when my mother could no longer care for herself. Mom had been a chronic alcoholic since forever and it was extremely difficult to see her in so much emotional and physical pain. I couldn't stop her from drinking, but I could arrange to keep her physically safe, and I had to know that was all I could do for her. When mom died, ten years ago, I realized that I wasn't mourning her passing, I was mourning her life.

How many of us have seen trouble brewing at work, and tried to jump in feet first, into a situation that was none of our business? That's the perfect scenario for a weapon. Sometimes it works well – but often it just becomes an unbelievable mess. Depends on the size of the weapon. We are paid to do a job, do it well, be proactive in our environment, offer assistance if needed (different than offering "help" during trouble), and be on time. These are some of the emotional skill sets we need to take into our work environment, and leave our baggage at home.

There's a Universal Principle that says "if you want help, you have to ask". That's a good mantra to keep on the back burner of our brains.

SELF-INDULGENCE or SELF NURTURING

(handwritten annotation: "escape")

A great many of us learn at a very early age that if we want something we had better get it now, because if we don't get it now, we may never get it.

If everybody in the family was tiptoeing around the big white elephant in the living room known as alcoholism, we were very often fortunate if we had a solid roof over our heads, food in our stomachs and clothes to wear to school. Any money that was left over went to support the habit of the alcoholic or drug abuser. We learned, therefore, that if we really wanted something and that something was offered to us, we had better get it now. Or we learned a way or ways of getting it as quickly as we could.

Coping mechanisms vary from family to family. Sometimes we coped by convincing ourselves that we were such bad children that we didn't deserve what we wanted anyway so that precious something ceased to have any meaning for us and we blocked it out of our minds. A lot of the time we were afraid to speak up and voice our needs and desires, so our families were never aware of them in the first place. For instance, if we wanted a pair of skates and there was never any money around for extras like skates, we told ourselves and everyone within hearing distance that we had no desire to learn to skate or play hockey.

If we wanted a bicycle to be able to get to and from school, and to ride with our friends (if we were lucky enough to have any) and there was never enough money for a bicycle, we would often put that out of our minds and in the same place that we put the pair of skates.

Until one day, some type of anger surfaces from the psyche that says "no, damnit, I want it and I'm going to get it – and I'm going to get it any way that I can".

If we wanted that bicycle bad enough and our anger was cold enough, and within our limited vision we see no other way of getting it, we will steal it. Or we will steal something else that we can fence to get the money to get the bicycle. We learn to cope with the only types of tools we have been given.

If our primary caregivers are wandering around in a chaotic state trying to figure out how they themselves are going to keep body and soul together while tiptoeing around the big white elephant there is little chance that they will notice that somewhere we have learned the skill of getting something for nothing.

And so it proliferates.

We get away with it once. We get away with it twice. We get away with it three times.

If, in fact, our mother does clue in, it very well may be that she is too tired, distraught, hung over, over-worked, battered, to address the issue of how we came about our new precious treasure. And so the circle continues, getting wider and more devious as we go along. We continue to create a set of circumstances that will allow us to obtain the things that most other kids we know seem to take for granted. And we continue to get more and more angry.

Why???

Because the items we are acquiring through manipulation, theft, and/or other means are not being acquired through healthy environments, and the circle of self-indulgence begins to form. If we had that bicycle, that pair of skates, that favourite doll, that perfect dress, those great jeans, life would be better.

Some of us try to work for our pocket money. And very often that helps for awhile. It helps until our grades start to suffer at school or until it becomes apparent that some of our hard earned money was needed to buy extra food or other essentials and we ended up back in square one.

We weren't able to obtain the object of our affection and frequently, when we did attain it, that object lay dormant because we didn't have the time or the energy to enjoy it.

And the rage continues to build. We continue to find means of stuffing it down so that we can survive.

So we continue in our childhood to act out our basic needs and to lay in wait until we can get the hell out of there.

For a lot of us that means quitting school, getting some sort of job, and buying our possessions on credit. For some of us it means hitting the streets at an early age, selling our bodies, dealing in drugs, make a quick buck, to get what we think we so desperately want. The acting out continues.

Two of the most important things parents are required to provide are safety and a nurturing environment. If we are dealing with the family disease of drug or alcohol dependency, each of these is stripped away.

I don't know if we ever totally recover from these issues. Even as I write this, I feel myself being drawn into the depths of my refrigerator to discover the delights of some rich and soothing chocolate that will make me feel better. Or so I think.

We may no longer be under the thumbs of our primary caregivers, but that doesn't mean that they do not have a profound influence on everything we do. If that were no longer the case, then we wouldn't be continually getting into debt, creating our own drug and alcohol problems, battling an eating disorder, dealing with self-imposed violence, finding a "strong man" who ends up beating the living shit out of us when he comes home drunk. Or alternatively, a sweet and gentle woman who turns out to have so many psychological problems that you wonder how the hell you missed them in the first place.

In each of these scenarios, we are acting out the roles of one or both of our parents.

The beat goes on.

We live in a self indulgent society. How many times a day do we see ads for fast food, fast cars, slick music, sexy clothes, great vacations, all of which are sold to us in the name of escape.

If we sit down and make a layman's analysis of the Madison Avenue Dance, how much of that stuff is really going to make us happy? Or fulfilled?

Well, we have to eat. We have to put a roof over our heads and clothes on our back. To obtain these, we have to work.

Do we want the extra stuff for escape or do we want it for pleasure?

How do we define pleasure and how do we define escape? There's a fine line between the two.

We can escape into that quart of chocolate ice cream because, for a moment, it is going to help us stuff our feelings, but will we derive any pleasure out of putting on our favourite pair of pants and not be able to zip them up?

We can buy an automobile that we can ill afford, that's loaded with everything, but will that automobile give us any pleasure while we are scrambling to make the monthly payments and perhaps have no money left over to buy gas, let alone any repairs that may be needed.

We can escape into our favourite watering hole on a Friday night after a tough week at work, to live, laugh and enjoy with our friends, but will we derive any pleasure from waking up on Saturday morning so hung over that the rest of the week-end is a total write-off.

This is a good way to define self indulgence. Self indulgence is synonymous with escape.

This is where we take a look at our escape mechanisms as children, and see how they fit into the coping mechanisms we develop as adults. And here is where we learn that we need to clean up our act.

It really is a never-ending story. I don't know if we attain all of the answers, but I do know that I can work this one, One Day at a Time. We begin to draw that fine line between self-indulgence and self-nurturing.

As children of an abundant planet, we deserve the best. We need to learn the tools to use to give us the best. Self-nurturing goes hand in hand with self-esteem.

As we begin to recognize ourselves in our human form as children of a Loving Universe, we begin to recognize that we are worth something and that, in fact, we are all contributors to the grand scheme. This makes it easier for us to take a look at ways to care for ourselves in a healthy manner.

There are as many ways to nurture ourselves as there are to be destructively self-indulgent. In fact, one balances out the other.

It is within each of us to discover our own worth, one step at a time. As we do so, our needs for destructive self-indulgence will begin to disappear, One Day at a Time.

We begin to see the nurturing process for what it really is, and we begin building little by little. This can be really difficult at first, because if we have never been nurtured, how do we nurture ourselves? We have to count to ourselves first, before we can count to anyone else. If we do it the other way around, we are doomed to fail.

Perhaps if we've been alcohol or drug dependent ourselves, we hit bottom and realize we have no place to go so we quit drinking and using. Perhaps, if we have been in a battering relationship, we realize there is no place to go but out, and we get out of it. We will not be battered if we know we don't deserve it.

If we carry around a large debt load and it has become extremely burdensome, we can methodically work to pay off those debts, not use credit cards, and one day wake up to realize that we have a sense of freedom sitting on our shoulders rather than a sense of burden.

This probably won't mean we will stay out of debt for the rest of our lives. However, through the learning process we are beginning to understand that debt can be used as a tool rather than a weapon.

Perhaps we will look at how we have been earning a living. If, for the last decade or so, we have been doing something that we absolutely loath doing, maybe it's time to bite the bullet, take a few night courses and do something that we know we will be good at.

The greatest gift that any of us can give ourselves is to be ourselves. We give ourselves this gift by nurturing ourselves.

We surround ourselves with people who honour us and our talents and idiosyncrasies. The people in our lives who have been hyper critical and condemning are people who are best left to their own devices. Because that's abuse. It's time we got away from it.

Part of the nurturing process is allowing others the right to their own journey. Each of us grows at a different pace, individually, yet coming together at specific points.

What works for me today may not work for you until next week. What works for you next week may never work for me at all.

Many of us have been so shut down from ourselves that we don't know how to get to that place of knowing. How do we get there? Think of it as something that you really, really want to do, that makes you feel better physically, mentally, and spiritually.

Yoga was my discipline of choice while going through this process. My mind became quiet, my body strong and supple, and my spirit wrapped itself around me and gave me contentment. Pure pleasure. I found yoga because I had tried everything else and I had no place left to go. Yoga also opened up very subtle pathways to unconscious memories. I discovered what real trust meant, and that it was OK to have healthy boundaries.

We look outside of ourselves for answers and then somehow that leads to inside of ourselves, and then somehow we make the connection. Isn't that cool??

This is all wonderful stuff but, when you are looking for that place, remember, IT ABSOLUTELY MUST BE A SAFE ENVIRONMENT!!!! Not every environment is safe, and this is where we need to learn discernment. We learn this by listening to our inner voice.

It sounds like all too much doesn't it? That's OK. We break it all down – One Day at a Time.

It's really important to make a list of body and soul self-nurturing techniques, by keeping yourself within yourself. Don't allow someone else to horn in on your very own, private territory.

We always know when we are not nurturing ourselves. We just have to tune in. If we are not self-nurturing we are overdosing on food, staying out too late, drinking too much, watching too much television, spending many hours at our computers, spending way too much money, skipping our exercise. You can add anything you like to this list. This is a daily monitoring process. We don't win every game we play with this, but we get better and better – One Day at a Time.

It's important that we all give up the idea that we have to look the part (whatever "the part" is) for friends, neighbours, strangers, co-workers. It's doubly important that we let our inner grace show through so that people notice us for the people we really are, and not for the facade we present to the world.

So, my suggestion to you is, sit down in a quiet corner with a pen and some paper, and make lists of twenty things that you really like to do, from the types of sporting events that you like to attend to the types of food you like to eat, to the type of physical discipline that you body responds to, to the type of entertainment you enjoy, to the kind of friends you like to be with.

Make a list from each of these and fill each one with twenty different variations on the theme.

Do I hear you say "I can't do that! I can't come up with twenty items for each of these!" You bet you can. Just think about it.

If you can't come up with it today, I guarantee you will come up with it tomorrow.

Now, the trick is, don't tell anyone you're doing this. It is 100 % guaranteed that you get more free advice than you know how to handle. Remember, this is for you – and no one else.

You need to know what's good for you. You are the only person that can do this. When you get it done, go to the next step.

Put the papers away for awhile. Perhaps a week. No shorter, but perhaps longer.

Take the papers out and re-read them.

Carefully look at the items you wrote on the paper. Now, prioritize them.

Choose one item from each of these pieces of paper.

Now promise yourself faithfully that you will do one of those items from each piece of paper. Now, go do them.

Some of your items will be free and some of them will cost some money. Again, think about it. Aren't you worth spending a little money on? I don't mean to the extent of your visa, but maybe one of those items is to visit the planetarium. OK. So spend Ten bucks and visit the planetarium. Maybe one of the items is better nutrition. OK. Eat an apple every day for a week. Carefully choose each of the seven apples, and keep them safe, just for yourself. Each of these two events will open up different avenues on your journey. And it's the start of living mindfully. (a whole other chapter).

You are now creating a journey for yourself. You can continue to create several journeys for yourself, and each of these journeys will teach you how to self-nurture, and that is one of the most fantastic journeys you will ever take in your entire life.

VULNERABILITY or NEEDINESS

The dictionary describes "vulnerable" as "open to attack or injury of a non-physical nature".

A description of "needy" is "... to be needful or necessary to a person or to some end or purpose...".

We talk quite a bit about vulnerability in this book, and how necessary that vulnerability is to our healing process. We also talk about how to protect our flanks while we are at our most vulnerable, so we don't find ourselves in positions of being attacked. Or, if we are attacked, we need to know that we have a place or places of refuge to help us through these difficult times.

Neediness is a whole different ball game.

How do we define these two very important terms?

Let's take each separately, and examine each one on its own merits.

Vulnerability

I think vulnerability is something we feel when we are healing. Healing anything, from a cut finger to a battered psyche. What we are really doing, I think, is feeling the beginnings of emotional health. Of course, we know we feel vulnerable when we are healing. When the pain comes up and the anger sets in, we shake, quake, cry, sleep, stay awake, eat, go hungry. We feel that if anyone looks at us sideways we are either going to scream or punch them in the chops. We learn to trust our support group, open up to a sponsor (this is vital), make our way in life with different rules.

We have learned that we feel vulnerable at other times in our lives as well. We feel hurt and vulnerable when someone hurts our feelings, at the end of a relationship, when a friend lets us down, when someone dies. Whenever there is a period of grief, vulnerability sets in.

And that's why vulnerability is synonymous with healing. We need to grieve something or someone to be healthy, and we are now allowing vulnerability to become part of an ongoing process.

An upside to vulnerability is that, generally, other people like us more. When we are willing to admit we are hurt or frightened, people often respond in a positive fashion. Especially if they know we are doing something about it.

An example of this is someone who gets up in front of a group of people and says, before she begins her talk "standing in front of all of you makes me feel very nervous...". When someone says that, we immediately begin to empathize, and our own survival barriers come down a little. We are willing to let her come nearer to us, because we know where she's coming from. Because, we've also taken risks, and the risks have left us with dangling nerve ends.

Neediness

Neediness, on the other hand, is a whole different ball game. Neediness is there when our denial walls are at their highest, and we are climbing out of ourselves to meet our inner needs. We are scared to death to look inwards, so we are constantly looking outwards. We think the only way we can be whole is by needing to be needed. We stay in a bad relationship because we think we are needed. We are always on the lookout for people we can rescue. If we can rescue someone, then they need us. And another vicious circle begins. Because we don't know we are being needy. We think we are being vulnerable.

Untreated co-dependents are really easy to spot. A woman is alone at a party, and she is constantly shifting her eyes over the men, regardless with whom she is speaking. If she sees someone she knows or thinks she would like to know, it's only a matter of time before she is glued at his side. And crying for attention. A highly co-dependent woman will read that attention any way she wants. The object of her desire may just be acting politely. She will immediately take it for more than it is, and decided that there really *is* a light in his eye after all. And the games begin. Women in high levels of denial, particularly attractive women, are constantly setting themselves up. And they find out the hard way, that the spark they see is directly attached to the area of the groin. Once the interests of this spark are served, it begins to fade. They are now rejected. They don't know why. And the circle of need starts up all other again. Time to go on to the next hostage.

Men set themselves up with unattainable women, as well. Looking for the same "clue", the clue that doesn't really exist for very long, only to be let down and left bleeding.

We must break the neediness and go into our vulnerability, and we do this when we begin addressing our issues.

The difference between neediness and vulnerability can be drawn by such a fine line we often miss the mark.

But, there is no other way. We just have to keep plugging at it. Because, we deserve better than what we've got, and we are going to get it.

As we begin setting up guidelines for ourselves, we can clue into the differences, and begin building healthy lives.

ACTION or REACTION

I don't think it is any great revelation to anyone that selfishness comes from reactive thinking. When we're brought up in a dysfunctional environment we learn at very early ages what reactive techniques we can use to get us out of very sticky situations. However, reactive thinking causes us to lose control.

We lose control of a situation, of a scenario, and ultimately our lives.

This comes in different degrees. We see it at a very personal level with how we react, externally or internally, with family members, particularly with family members who are still living in their pain, and we see it throughout our North American culture.

Sometimes we react by not acting at all.

Sometimes we react by putting a gun in our hands and shooting at someone because they have a different belief system, different skin, or a better pair of Nikes. It's all a matter of degree.

In today's world reading the newspaper can be an extremely painful experience. We can feel helplessness and rage at what is happening to a society that we are members of and we, in turn, begin to react in ways that are familiar to us.

We can react by withdrawing. We can react by lashing out. But react we do.

The way to act within the confines of our own lives is by allowing ourselves the freedom to work through our own stuff and ultimately create an environment that allows us to be actors on our own stage. And we very often miss the mark.

We must not continue to beat ourselves up!! That reaction trigger we all carry around with us can and must be stopped. If we give ourselves ten seconds before reacting, we can respond.

That Committee of Assholes that runs around inside each of our heads is, by far, made up of the most vicious group of enemies that any of us will ever meet.

This Committee, the enemy, that allows us to pile hurt upon hurt and react within that circle, keeps right on reacting.

The first thing we need to do is forgive this Committee. The second thing we need to do is forgive the people around us who we see as being hurtful, and the third thing we need to do is get on with it. And by getting on with it we begin to take action.

Although the action is painful, it's healthy. The reaction is also painful, but it is hurtful. If we respond we are only going to act for healthy reasons. If we react we are going to react out of illness. The choice is our own.

Sometimes, as we continue our journey, we get into these reactive situations and ways of thinking that perpetuates the ego self and the Committee of Assholes begins to become our own enemy within. I don't know many people who haven't said "I am my own worst enemy". We can all relate. To be our own worst enemy we have to place ourselves in reactive situations on a chronic basis.

Certainly there are reactive situations that are healthy. These are the important times when we need to be able to respond.

If we are at a lake and see a swimmer in trouble, our first reaction is to help the person. Our second reaction is a response. What can we do? If you can't swim, don't go in after them. What is around us that we can get to that person? Maybe all we need to do is keep yelling for help.

If we are the first ones to arrive on the scene of an accident, and someone has been badly hurt, we can only react to our knowledge of first aid. For instance, if we are not aware that moving someone can permanently damage their spinal cord, we could tug and pull at them, creating more damage. Our response could be to keep them stable and warm, and in turn, send for professional help.

But what about the reactive situations we find ourselves in on a daily basis? The trick is to recognize them, and teach ourselves to respond. That isn't always easy.

The best way to recognize reactive situations is by recognizing our own level of recovery and knowledge. Every day, somewhere, somehow, something is going to come up that will cause us to react in a certain way. We will react or respond to that situation through enlightenment or from denial.

It depends of where we are, physically, emotionally, mentally. If we react to someone who has heavy control issues and we have dealt with some of our own control issues, it's not too tough to just step aside.

We can do this in various ways. We can literally step aside and do nothing and the person with the control issues will do one of two things. She will attack from another angle or she will find someone else to play in her sandbox. If she finds someone else to play in her sandbox then it's no longer our problem. If she comes at us from a different angle, we can react with the knowledge that we have on hand.

One way to stop the attack is to ask, in a neutral voice, "would you like to explain that further?" "Tell me what you mean".

Now we've bounced the ball back into her court. She didn't expect that and we are now in a position to watch for her reaction because we are beginning to respond.

This can be really difficult to do. This is a tool I continue to learn on a daily basis. My immediate reaction to being verbally abused is "flight or fight". That's how I was raised. Sometimes flight works. Fighting never works.

A lot of people have learned to be abusive in a very civilized manner. We see it all around us. It's really easy to throw in an innuendo, a hurtful comment, a backstabbing remark to a co-worker or another friend that will strip your carcass bare and leave the bones to dry in the sun.

If that person is coming at us from our own dysfunctions and in a way that triggers our own memory banks it is an extremely difficult project to set ourselves up in a way we can deal with.

Haven't you laid awake at nights thinking about the time that your Aunt Sadie, your boss, Mr. Smith, said such-and-such and if you only had the opportunity now, at this time, you would know exactly what to say? Of course you would. You've had time to process it and get some detachment. Somebody in your Committee of Assholes has given you what is perceived to be an appropriate answer.

But, is it the appropriate answer? More often than not, if we haven't dealt with the issues that need to be dealt with, it isn't. And that's the secret.

I doubt any of us will ever be in a position to go through life and not respond on a daily basis to something that is happening. And that's the lesson – to respond appropriately. We only do this as we learn to use the tools that would belong to an emotionally healthy person. It is an ongoing process, a day by day experience, that we have to look at, examine, and redefine and NOT BEAT OURSELVES UP.

Of course we are going to make mistakes. That is all part of the game.

If we were perfect people we wouldn't have to be in this school called a lifetime, we'd just be too busy learning how to surf in the clouds.

All too often we don't give ourselves credit for the times we respond in a positive and healthy way. We push those to the side, almost like negating our own growth, and continue to concentrate on unhealthy reactions that we continue to deal with. That is so silly. We all do it, and it's really silly.

Our Committees of Assholes continue to tell us that we were "bad" people when we don't react the way the Committee thinks we should react. We need to learn to quiet the Committee and respond. We simply must stop attacking ourselves the way we perceive other people attacking us.

We have to go beyond being survivors and into beings of wellness.

It is an overwhelming proposition. It is a huge job. So, how do we keep from allowing it to overwhelm us? Easy. One Day at a Time.

Each of us has a right to be counted. Each of us has a right to be recognized. Each of us has a right to be free.

None of us has the right to place our value systems and beliefs in the path of someone else and expect them to pick it up and run with our ball. That is absolute nonsense.

It can become as simple as driving your car. A car is a valuable tool to get us from point A to point B. Before we get into this tool, this car, we have to learn to use it. We have to learn to react accordingly.

There are rules and regulations on the road to allow other cars the same type of access that we have. To allow bicycles safe pedaling along certain pathways, and to allow pedestrians to cross certain intersections. These rules and regulations are made up to place us in positions of safety so that we can reach our destinations relatively unscathed and relaxed.

Does everyone follow them? Not on your life. No pun intended.

Every day we are bombarded with stories of traffic accidents that cost thousands of dollars, leave bodies disfigured, minds empty, lives altered forever, and people dead. Why? Because somebody, somewhere, has reacted, and reacted in a very negative fashion. The result has been carnage.

Wouldn't it be great if for one day in our cities and towns everybody obeyed every traffic law? People would get to and from work on time and refreshed. There would be no broken bones or bent fenders. No one would be in a morgue. Insurance rates wouldn't be going up. Cars would last longer. Roads would be safer. People would be healthier. Life would be easier. Does this ever happen? I've never heard of it. Not once. Each time I get into my car I expect that I am going to have to react. And I am either going to have to react as a driver or as an observer. It depends on the circumstances at the time. As a driver, I am going to have to react to the guy ahead of me who slams on his brakes. If I have been tailgating, my reaction is going to be too little, too late, and I'm going to plow into his rear end. If I've been following the rules of the road and he slams on his brakes, he and I are both going to be able to stop without damaging each other's vehicles.

If I see a green light ahead of me, and that green light is turning orange, I have two choices. I can either stop, or I can go. It depends on the intersection and how close I am to the amber light. I have a lot better chance of stopping the car if a child darts in front of me if I am obeying the traffic signals in a playground zone and not going over the posted speed limit. The child and I would be a little shook up, but neither of us would be damaged.

And I sure have a lot better chance of surviving if I don't have any booze or drugs in my system. Everyone knows people who drink and drive. Everyone. There are no exceptions. What's the limit?

I think that the reactions we have when driving our cars are great learning tools for how we drive our lives.

The ability to drive a car is a privilege that the majority of us take for granted. To react in a negative way with that privelege can be equated to how we react within ourselves, and ultimately react with other people.

Action always comes down to choice. Most of us have absolutely no idea that we have as many choices as we do. We put on our blinkers and do a lot of stuff by rote, end up being tired and discouraged, and react accordingly. It's important to define our choices. We need to take a look at them and see where our choices are taking us. The more choices we have, the more we will give ourselves the opportunity to act within a given situation in a healthy way, rather than reacting negatively, ultimately doing harm to ourselves and those around us.

There's lots of theories about why violence is so prevalent in our society, and why many of our streets have become unsafe. My feeling is that people feel boxed in, are angry, and are lashing out. (reacting).

What can we do about it?

We can do the best that we can do for ourselves, examine our own choices, and get on with it. Doesn't that sound selfish? I suppose, to an extent, it does. For those of us with children it has made us more aware of the value of teaching choices to our own children so they they don't get stuck in the same box. I can't do this unless I look at my own choices, examine them, move forward, and act on those choices, rather than reacting to a situation over which I have no control.

We can make choices as a long term goal, and we can make choices on a daily basis. Now we are beginning to respond.

So, we have a choice. And only we make that choice.

This is a really good place to take out that pad of paper and that pen and start writing down choices.

If something is happening in your life right now and you don't know which way to act or respond, take a piece of paper, draw a line down the centre of it, put "positive" on the left and "negative" on the right, or the other way around if you like, and make a list on both sides of the paper. What can be the positive outcomes and what can be the negative outcomes? If you are having trouble compiling the list from an objective point of view put it away for a couple of days, pull it back out, take another look, and you will find that your subconscious has been working away on your list. You will be able to add to one or both sides of the paper. You will be amazed at what you discover, and what you need to do to make a healthy decision about a particular choice. Again, it's important that you don't tell anybody that you are doing this because you are going to get a whole lot of uncalled for advice. Unless it directly concerns a spouse or a child, do it on your own.

Put everything down that you can think of. Examine your list carefully. I can assure you that if you do this from a level of detachment, one side of the list will be longer than the other. From that vantage point it is a lot easier to make your choice.

You don't need to be influenced by what other people tell you. Certainly, other people can offer valuable information and make valid comments, and certainly those comments and that information can be drawn into your list. But it's also important for you to keep in mind that those people are not living inside your skin and the ultimate choice is yours.

<u>Sometimes our choice is not to make a choice.</u> And that's OK. Because, maybe, at the place we are at at any given time, it doesn't feel right to make a choice. If that, in fact, is right for you, then just leave it alone. When the time is right, you will know. And only you will know. No one else will be able to influence your choice because you will know what you are doing is right for you.

Keep up with this process until you feel comfortable with your list.

The more choices we have, the less we feel stuck, the less angry we are. The less angry, the less rage we have to contend with. The less rage, the less we have to deal with those negative-reactive behavior patterns.

Try it. What have you got to lose?

BUILDING WALLS or CREATING BOUNDARIES

I'd like to start this chapter with a metaphor. When we start building walls around us we do it for protection. We build brick by painful brick. Each brick is carefully mortared and put into place, and as each hurt and injustice is piled upon us, we methodically continue to build the bricks around ourselves.

If we look carefully at the bricks we can see that each brick is made up of anger, hate, deceit, lies, accusations, denial, and all that negative stuff. And because all of this stuff is so negative, when something happens that begins to tear at a part of this wall, it will cave in on us and hurt us even more.

The higher the walls of anger and betrayal, the more we become injured.

As we learn, through recovery, to take down these walls, to deal with our feelings, to work through the anger, we also become more aware of how totally defenseless we are. It doesn't feel like a great place to be. So, we need to create boundaries.

We can equate the boundaries to tent pegs. If you have ever had the experience of going camping and you've got a tent that is, say, nine by nine, it might have had a pole in the middle and a post at each corner, and here you are in the centre of this tent trying to put up the centre poll, so you can place the pegs, and you have never done it before, it can be really frustrating. (I understand that today's tents are more streamlined than this – but please bear with me.)

The worst thing that can happen is that the tent will fall down on your head. But, wonderful news, when the tent falls on your head, it doesn't hurt like the brick wall does. It is a lot easier to get up off the ground, put your hands over your head, push the canvas away, place the centre pole where it belongs, find the tent flap and go out and stake the pegs.

The pegs need to be of a sturdy material. The rope that entwines the pegs needs to be equally as sturdy, and we need to have the ability to attach the pegs to the rope. When all that is done, we now have a firmly placed tent. If it does fall in on us again, we will certainly feel uncomfortable for awhile but we will not be unduly bruised or damaged.

That's the metaphor.

We only know how to fight or flight. And we have to change that.

By building our wall of anger, deceit and denial, it is inevitable that we are going to suffer some incredible damage once, twice, three times, more, as we go through life. We cannot escape it. And we can't go back and forth between the brick walls and the tent with any comfort, either. We can't say to ourselves "well, that's all right. I'll just keep the brick house over here and I'll put the tent over there, and when I need the brick house I'll hop into it and I'll be safe, and when I think I am going to be placed in an awkward position, I'll just run over to the tent and I will use that instead.

It doesn't work that way.

Those of us who come from a background of denial think that we are safe in our brick and mortar house, and periodically we will open a small crack and allow someone in. And then, do you know what we do? We allow them into our own small space, our bubble, and we let it all hang out.

Because we are putting out energy that attracts like energy (the Laws of Attraction) we are really leaving ourselves wide open, and it is only a matter of time until we find ourselves in some incredible mess and again we begin asking "how did I get into this?" Easy. We didn't have any boundaries. We only had walls. Sometimes the bricks come down and hit us in the head, or hit us in the gut, and sometimes, if we get angry enough, we start throwing some of those bricks back at whomever has harmed us, because we didn't have the knowledge and the will to build the boundaries that we need to protect ourselves.

And the cycle begins again. And the cycle is vicious. We allow it to continue because that is all we know. And what is abnormal becomes normal. We continue to act out our lives rather than to respond within our lives.

How do we change this?

We have to learn to use the tent. When we are passing from the brick walls into the boundaries of the tent, is when we are the most vulnerable. And that is the scariest part. However, it gets easier to build boundaries as our self-esteem grows.

When we can say we are worthy because of our belief systems, because we are a child of the Universe, because we are the direct product of the handiwork of God, not only does it make for humility, it also gives us strength.

We are not going to get that tent right the very first time we try, but it is much easier to keep working away at it, and that causes much less pain, than when we build walls.

Let's look at some practical ways of doing this.

It is not an uncommon occurrence, in fact, it's almost the norm, for co-dependent adults to meet someone that they are attracted to, and within the first twenty-four hours, tell them their whole life story. John Bradshaw used to tell a wonderful story about this, where he admits to telling the other person every little secret in his life, on first meeting, and at four o'clock in the morning, as they were parting company, saying to the other person "by the way, I also screwed a chicken when I was twelve years old".

If the other person is a healthy individual, that person will disappear and you will probably never hear from him/her again. If the other person is also a co-dependent, he/she will be just as intrigued with that story as he/she can be, and say "gee, this person is really fascinating, I want to see him/her again". And so the dance begins.

I was at a dinner party one night with a group of single people. We had been brought together to see how we liked each other, and to help us all widen our circle of friends. I remember watching myself from the perspective of where I am now to the perspective of where I was before I started recovery. There weren't many similarities.

The first thing I noticed was that I really enjoyed myself. I kept thinking of this evening as a three hour vacation with new people I had never met before, and if I so chose, I would never see them again. And from that vantage point I was able to be me. I was able to express my views, have a good laugh, and stop a lech in his tracks. I also noticed that my antennae was really up. Without even being conscious of what I was doing, I had placed a specific focus on each individual at the table and I had looked for clues as to their personality traits, their biases, likes and dislikes.

It wasn't intense, it just happened.

The gentleman to my left was very quiet, very perceptive and spent the night drinking coke. During the few minutes of conversation between us, I learned that he was a recovering alcoholic and had some definite views on living one day at a time.

The woman sitting across from him was extremely self-absorbed and rigid, very concerned with her appearance and actions. She left early.

The gentleman across from me was the lech who was having the devil of a time controlling the amount of alcohol he was consuming while he was hitting on all of the women at the table.

Another woman was so nervous that all she could talk about was her kids, and her work, and everyone was getting pretty bored.

I had a chance to spend some time with that woman after the dinner and I discovered a whole other side to her. She was very knowledgeable, very intuitive, and a lot of fun. I felt badly for her, because no one else at the table saw this side to her.

The man to my right was still in the process of grieving the death of his wife. He had very definite views on the roles that men and women should play in our culture and loved his children very much.

I wasn't aware that I was assimilating all this information until I began to take a look at the evening from the vantage point of the morning after. I also began to wonder what my dinner companions thought about me. Obviously the recovering alcoholic zeroed in on a common bond. The woman who was so nervous felt comfortable enough to show me the side of her that was truly wonderful. I also learned that I really didn't care what most people thought. I did, however, care that I had made contact with one or two people who, given other circumstances, would perhaps enrich my life.

I couldn't help the man who was grieving the death of his wife. He had to go through his own pain his own way. And that was a new experience. I didn't want to fix him. Ten years before, I would have wanted to fix him – and it would have ended really badly.

The lech would have also been a challenge. I would have shown him! Who did he think he was? Did he ever need to learn a thing or two! I discovered that I had zero interest in ever seeing this person again, because he had absolutely nothing to do with my reality.

This was progress!! I was learning to respond to my life instead of reacting in it!!

The changes are both subtle and painful. Never easy, always worthwhile. I can't tell you I was really good at it, because I had to work it one day at a time, but I am better at it now – because I am better. And that's the difference.

It is, I think, almost impossible to break down that brick and mortar wall that we build around ourselves without the help of a very fine support system. As we begin to feel safe, we can start to tear down all of that crap we have been building around ourselves, brick by painful brick, look at our issues, work through them, and step out into the world as a healthy individual.

We all know that we desperately want to say "I can do it today", but we can't. If I heard it once, I swear I heard it a thousand times, "I want to be well, and I want to be well, now". But it's not that easy, it is just part of the journey.

We can't reach that place of self awareness if we don't know the self. We can't build the boundaries if we don't know what we truly want deep within our souls.

We can't get to any of these places until we know who we are. It is impossible. As long as we continue to posture, to ingratiate, to shock, to act out, to manipulate, that is what we get in return. It is that Universal Principle of The Law of Attraction.

Much of the bricks and mortar is buried so deeply within our psyches that it can take years to work through it all, to break it all away, to get it all out. We have to continue to do it. It is an absolute must not only for ourselves but for those we love.

Another interesting thing about boundaries is that we are given the opportunity to expand them or shrink them, depending on the situation.

Within a group of strangers, it is very acceptable to only expose a small amount of ourselves.

We need to learn how to expand or contract our boundaries in all sorts of relationships, whether it be with a mate, children, siblings, parents, cousins, aunts, uncles, whatever. We can extend the boundaries or draw them in, depending on the person involved and the circumstances surrounding the relationship.

It is important to remain flexible with our boundaries. Sometimes stuff we think we should know is absolutely none of our business. And that works with family members and loved ones wanting more information about us. We are always truthful and authentic, we just learn where to draw that line.

As we recognize our own boundaries it becomes easier to recognize the other person's wall or boundaries, see it for what it is and not internalize that person's stuff, and that leaves us less wounded. See how it works?

One reason that it appears to be easy to jump from the walls to the tent is because each of us has so many facets to our personality. Many parts make up the whole. One facet of our personality will allow us to enter the tent with relative ease, and another will keep us caged behind the wall.

It is the parts of us that are caged that require the work. If we stick to the easy parts we don't continue to grow. I think that is one of the reasons we have adversities in our lives. Adversities teach us how to break down those brick walls in that particular part of our personalities so we can create our boundaries. The tougher it is the more we know this is where we have to do the work.

It is really easy to create boundaries in a comfortable or even semi-comfortable environment. It's a hell of a lot more difficult to break down the walls when we are feeling extremely uncomfortable, and defensive. That's usually what happens in a family unit.

We will find ourselves in a situation of adversity, usually around illness or denial, or both, where there are walls up all over the place. Not only are we dealing with our own walls, but we are also trying to deal with the other person's wall as well, and the fur really starts to fly.

Instead of letting the negative energy out so we can dissipate it, it keeps coming back at an even greater force than it left us, and it creates this vicious circle that can be extremely difficult to break. I call that circle "denial".

Healthy communication creates boundaries. Fight or flight builds walls.

There are, of course, certain circumstances when a type of flight is acceptable. Working environments are fraught with all sorts of issues. If we have our boundaries in place, we will recognize signs that colleagues and co-workers give out that spell "danger".

Every working environment has that, and the trick is to learn to sidestep those issues, rather than confronting them, so that we can keep our boundaries intact and get on with our jobs. Most people who are out for blood eventually spill their own and it doesn't make a lot of sense to be in the line of fire.

Within the family unit, we are looking at different dynamics. If we are dealing with a family member who has a high level of denial in a certain area of his/her life, and we have tried to reach that person through those layers, and that person refuses to be reached, the very best tool that we have is the Serenity Prayer. "Grant me the grace to accept the things I cannot change...".

One of the things that has happened in my own family is that those of us who are in recovery are working at different levels. What is working for me now isn't necessarily working for another family member. What is working for that family member isn't necessarily working for me. That can sometimes bring us to cross purposes.

If the boundaries are established and the love and respect for each other is there, then confrontation can be a healthy way to dissipate the disruption that is happening in our lives. I don't believe that confrontation should, in any way, be reactionary. I believe that confrontation needs to be intuitive and loving.

You can be angry as hell at someone and confront your loved one in an intuitive and caring manner. An argument may ensue, but by keeping the argument in the "I factor", in other words, not laying any blame at their feet, but explaining how you feel, most often it will end with an amicable solution.

I still have a lot of problems with confrontation. Confrontation to me means violence, and I can find more ways than God made little green apples to justify why I do not want to confront a member of my family whom I love very much about a certain issue that has reared its ugly head. I am still working on that point in my own recovery where

I will become good at this. And I know that this is one of the bricks that I have to seriously take a look at in my own walling system, so that I break it down and move on to the tent, and create the boundaries with the tent pegs.

If I don't do that, I will not only fail myself, but I am sure to fail the other person, and we will both end up losing.

That is the tragedy. If we both lose, and don't continue to do the work that's necessary to break that cycle, then that cycle remains generational and it will continue to ferment down through some sort of genetic structure, from generation to generation.

It's the old saw isn't it?

There is no way around it. You can only go through it. Food for thought? You bet! Worth while? Every bit of it!

We cannot change the world, we can only change ourselves.

OBSESSION or DISCIPLINE

(handwritten annotations: "unrealistic to behavior or reward unpenetrable" – "brittle walls"; "focusing on solutions + positive change")

Everyone needs discipline. We cannot have courage without it.

Discipline comes in many forms, types, sizes, interests and needs.

Discipline helps us earn a living, and enables us to achieve feelings of well-being during leisure pursuits. It is a very valuable tool and we cannot live a productive and happy life without it.

If we want to become an IT specialist, we need the discipline to go to school, spend hours of frustrating time at computers, and have a lot of patience. Eventually we get that degree.

If we want to play a mean game of tennis, we start at an early age to learn to handle a tennis racket, make a good serve, hit the ball over the net and make our opponent sweat. That gives us a feeling of well-being for our bodies and our minds.

Discipline gives us peace of mind. If we use a discipline to learn meditation, yoga, tai chi, or any number of Eastern philosophies, we begin to notice that as we are working with our bodies in a very methodical, careful, spiritual way, our minds aren't racing around as much, we have a general feeling of well-being, and we just feel better.

All of these types of disciplines help to feed our own trilogies and they are absolutely vital to our emotional and physical well-being.

Unfortunately, when we are raised in a dysfunctional environment, discipline is usually the last thing on our minds Fight or flight often comes first. Don't talk, don't trust, don't feel. That's the name of the game. Or we use a discipline to escape a situation rather than address a situation. A discipline can become an obsession if we use it that way.

Is that necessarily bad? Let's do some exploring with this one.

I think it is necessary, at times in our lives, to use disciplines in an obsessive fashion.

Olympic athletes certainly need it. Watch the figure skaters the next time you see it advertised on TV. These young athletes didn't get that degree of poise, perfection and control by an hour or two of discipline a day. Their days often begin about 4:00 am. They have coaches to study with, compulsory figures to learn, long hours of practice, injuries to sustain. They must learn and maintain endurance. Perhaps they will study ballet on the "side" to teach them the art of being graceful, as well as strong. And somewhere through all of this they are keeping up with school. These young people need to work very hard for many, many years. They have to look at their failures and turn them into successes.

They are constantly surrounded by people who help to feed that inner core of strength that says "I can do it", and they can and do spend many, many hours alone perfecting their craft. And maybe, if the gods are with them, one day they will participate in the Olympics. And if they participate in the Olympics, maybe, just maybe, they will win that gold. And maybe they will be given a contract with a major ice show and endorsements to sign for major sports wear manufacturers, and they can begin reaping the benefits of their obsessive discipline. Maybe. But they hold on to that dream to prove to themselves, before anyone else, that they have what it takes. They will give it everything they've got, so they can have the glory, and then get the fame.

Once the hard work of major competition is behind them, and if they have a healthy perspective on their lives, that obsessive discipline can now be altered to "discipline". The hours are still long, but the rewards can now be there. They can spend some time on play.

And then again, maybe not. It all depends on how each of these young people views his/her obsession.

Lots of people who are obsessed do work that is absolutely crucial to humankind. Without them we would have tubed the planet long ago, instead of being given this one last chance to finally get it right.

Dr. Jonas Salk was obsessed while he was searching for a vaccine for polio. Alexander Graham Bell suffered huge bouts of long hours and insomnia while he was figuring out how to invent the telephone. Albert Einstein spent many thousands of hours on his theory of relativity.

We can only hope and pray that people that obsessed are now working around the clock for ways of disarming nuclear warheads, creating fuel that is totally friendly to the environment, feeding the planet's millions of starving, cleaning up our oceans and rivers, re-building eroded top soil, creating world peace. We can only hope.

There is a saying in AA that says "Stick with the Winners".

If we stick with the winners, our lives are bound to improve. I think winning or losing definitely falls into this category of discipline or obsession. The trick is to know where to draw the line.

All of us have heroes. And most of our heroes are people who are obsessed with something.

My favourite hero is a man named Rick Hansen. Rick is a Canadian who was involved in a traffic accident when he was 15 years old. The traffic accident left him a paraplegic. He was in hospital for a long time. When he was released he went back to school and on to University. He was the first person in a wheel chair to graduate from the School of Physical Education at the University of British Columbia. While Rick was at University he was playing on the wheelchair basketball team and began to train competitively for marathons. Rich went on to win 19 international wheelchair marathons prior to his world tour. Rick Hansen was and is a world class athlete, in more ways than one.

Why?

While he was winning marathons he also had a dream. Not much was known about spinal cord injuries, or physical disabilities. However, with the medical techniques available today, many more people were now surviving disabling accidents.

Why not do a "Man in Motion" tour? Travel around the world from a wheelchair? That way, people would become more aware of the need for spinal cord research and the need for wheel chair bound people to be able to enter offices, restaurants, washrooms. People with disabilities could then participate fully in their own communities.

Rick's physical condition was superb from his competitive training, but he also began to consider the mental and emotional rigors that lay ahead. So, he began to train his mind as well.

He formed a group of people to travel with him. He sought corporate sponsorship to help pay for the cost. He never gave up on his dream. He finally started.

People didn't pay much attention to Rick for quite a while. But, he never gave up. He kept on going. He burned 271 calories for each hour he wheeled. The average number of wheel strokes per day numbered 45,000. He wore out over 200 wheelchair tires, traveled through 34 countries. He suffered through injuries, illness and fatigue. And he kept right on going. He just refused to quit.

After being away from home for eighteen months and two days, Rick finally ended back on Canadian soil. He only had to wheel across Canada now. A piece of cake. Only 13,661 kilometers to go to see all of Canada. It took him 9 months. He tried to travel an average of 70 miles a day. The momentum was building. People were now paying too much attention to him. It was slowing him up. He was gracious to everyone. Even though it meant he was going to have to wheel through the winter. He kept going. He never gave up. Finally, he made it back to Vancouver to a hero's welcome. People from all over Vancouver were downtown that day. People were openly weeping on the street as he wheeled by. People were surging around him, just to touch his chair, just so they could say that they touched their hero. Rick was home. In the end he had raised $23 Million Dollars for spinal cord research, wheelchair sports, rehabilitation and awareness. He had brought the physical needs of people with disabilities into the consciousness of the world. It was very, very successful.

After Rick got home, he married his physiotherapist, Amanda Reid, who had been on the tour with him, and they now have grown children. He wrote a book called "Man in Motion". He is working at the University. He does his daily workout and has turned his obsession into a discipline that is carrying him through his life. He continues to raise many millions of dollars for spinal chord research.

Rick is a wonderful inspiration.

Once, in an interview, I heard Rick tell a reporter that his parents encouraged him to strive to be a winner. Not a winner at sports, but a winner at life.

I don't know anyone who has been able to accomplish this as well as Rick. And that is why Rick is my hero.

When things get tough, I think of Rick. Would Rick quit? Have I finished my task? If I haven't finished my task, and I'm still doing it to the best of my ability, should I quit? Would Rick quit? Then the questions becomes, "is the compulsion and obsession worth it?"

It depends on the work at hand. And the attitude. What do I have to gain? What do I have to lose? What does the community have to gain – or lose? Do I keep on going?

These are questions we all have to ask ourselves at least once during our lives. Just because we've done our pain work, does not mean we are finished with our life work. It just means we have more tools.

One of these tools now is that line between our obsession and our discipline. Can we examine it and know what it is? Are we capable of knowing the difference?

Everyone knows that it is essential to exercise a minimum of three times a week to help keep the body healthy for a lifetime. Everyone knows that. How many people do that?

Everyone knows that it is essential to eat a healthy diet. Everyone knows that. How many people do that?

Everyone knows we need discipline at work. We need to be punctual, polite, trustworthy, professional. Everyone knows that. How many people do that?

It is a monitoring process.

Did you get your exercise this week? If not, why not? Did you give up? Why? What would it take for you to begin again?

How is your diet? Do you still eat too much sugar and carbohydrates? Yes? No? If yes, what would it take for you to give up sugar and carbs for just one day? How much?

Have you been thinking about starting or completing a project? Where are you in this journey? Have you set goals that you can meet? If not, why not? What will it take for you to meet just one of those goals?

That's discipline.

Again, the trick is to know when to give something up and let it go. Most of us Adult Children never learned healthy discipline at home. It takes us longer to get in touch with the fine points.

We have to prove to ourselves (and only ourselves) that our lives are a lot better with healthy discipline than they are without it.

That takes time. We don't do it overnight. In the meantime, these fight or flight tapes are playing away in our heads. Which way do we jump?

We jump right into a support group, that's where we jump. When in doubt jump into a support group. First rule of recovery.

Don't try and go it alone.

No support group? Form one.

If that old tape gets stuck on "repeat" and we can't get it unstuck, we are going to do something really unhealthy. But we've done our pain work. We already know that – don't we? Not always, not all the time. Remember, we never recover. We can only check in and improve.

Support. Our answer always lies in support.

Let's take a look at obsessive behaviour gone bad. An athlete starts at an early age to be the best he can be. He likes to lift weights. Besides, it gets him away from his family of origin. And he has some peace and quiet. The gym is a lot more quiet than the fights at home. Pretty soon, he doesn't feel so helpless. And he can see where his muscles in his arms and legs are becoming more delineated. Not only is his body hard, but his mind isn't spinning quite as much. This is great. Someone at the gym tells him this could be even greater. All he has to do is take these pills and keep up the good work, and those muscles are not only going to be more delineated, but they are really going to bulge, and no one, but no one is ever going to be able to push him around again. He begins taking them. And they work. He works out obsessively, day in and day out. He lives in that gym. His main meal becomes these little pills. He watches himself get larger and larger. His body becomes his own tank. He feels invincible. There are some side effects beginning to appear from these little pills, but he ignores them. Because look at him. He's like a Greek God! Invincible. Nobody can stop him. Besides, if he just keeps obsessively lifting those weights, those side effects will go away. Those things only happen to other people, anyway.

Steroids now become a way of life. The discipline has become an obsession, and the steroids become the only answer to the body beautiful. Just like the alcoholic who takes that drink to feel better. Same reasons. Different drug.

If he is lucky he will only get sick and then be able to get his life back. If he's not lucky, he will die.

You be the judge.

How do you want to orchestrate your own discipline? Because, with discipline comes freedom. It is an easy rule, keep it clean and honest and within your own grasp. That is where the fine line is.

SURVIVOR (FOREGIVENESS) or VICTIM

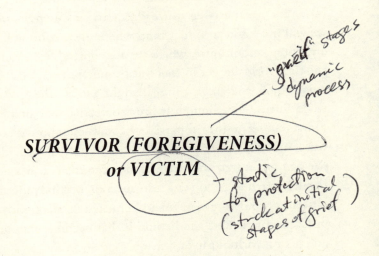

There will always be people around us who press our buttons It is not only a fact of life, but a Universal Truth that says this is one of the ways we learn about our own issues. If we are fortunate, and we have done some pain work, we have been in recovery for awhile and we are into a group that has supported us, we begin to recognize what these situations call for. This also becomes the product for forgiveness. When we know that we are really mirroring ourselves in other people, we can let those people go. This is not always easy. Sometimes it takes a great deal of work, but we know this is what we have to do.

Once we start to deal with our issues on our own personal level, and begin to get a lot of those issues behind us, the people around us change. Our buttons don't get pressed as often as before. Life begins to be easier in many respects and the button pushers in our lives are more easily recognized. This is a time when our group work and our journals become all important. If she is pushing buttons in us but we don't recognize that part of our pain work, we will not know or understand where she is coming from, and more importantly, where we are coming from. This is the time for us to get in touch with our feelings, intuition, compassion, so that we can really take a look. The only way to do this is by being totally impartial. And that ain't easy. However, out of this impartiality comes one more piece of the giant jigsaw puzzle that makes each of us an individual. We can put it into the vacant spot, according to where we think it needs to be, do our introspection on that particular button, do our forgiveness and compassion work with the other person, leave them behind if that becomes necessary, and get on with our lives.

Sound easy? Well, the steps are relatively easy; sometimes the work is difficult.

The issue of forgiveness is the most important work that we will ever do. Fortunately, or unfortunately, depending on your point of view, forgiveness work requires a lot of pain work. To get to it, you have to go through it. There is no way around it, over it, under it, beside it, or anything like that. It just doesn't work that way.

Some people in the metaphysics community may tell you otherwise. Some people will tell you that all you have to do is just get yourself into a nice quiet place and repeat the words "I forgive my mother (father) (whomever). I forgive them and let them go. I set them free". And that is certainly part of the process.

Until we have dealt with our pain and our anger, we cannot get to that place of forgiveness that any of the scriptures talk about because we don't understand what it is that we are forgiving. Sometimes it is enough to know that victims are the victims of victims. However, as children we tend to personalize everything around us and we continue to act within those very definitive roles that we set up for ourselves as kids so we can survive.

John Bradshaw's work on this, in my opinion, is the most valuable work that anyone has done. His book, **Homecoming**, defines all of our childhood developmental needs and explains why we will screw up if those needs have not been met.

Our pain work, in this context, is the most valuable work we can do for ourselves. And do it we must.

If we do not do this work, what has been happening in our lives will continue to happen. That jerk that was in your life that you now have finally been able to get rid of, is going to keep reappearing in your life. With another face, with another name, in another gender, perhaps, and another environment. But that jerk will continue to reappear. And that jerk will still be reappearing until we finally figure out what it is within us that keeps attracting these jerks.

This is why there is no way that we can sidestep the issue(s) of our own pain. We simply must go through it.

How many times has each one of us seen ourselves and someone we love, walk away from one really bad marriage, and climb right back in to another really bad marriage. The inventories of the spouses involved will have more similar personality patterns than we care to admit. Often, for instance, we will hear women say "I simply did not know that he was violent. He treated me so well while we were going together". Another really famous one is "I didn't know that he had a drinking problem". Or "Boy, this guy is really unavailable". (Married) (lives in another country) (been really hurt/damaged and wants no more involvement with anyone).

For those of us who have wrestled with co-codependency for most of our lives (and who among us hasn't?) this trap is ready for us to fall into. All of us seem to have an "ism" in our life, whether it's alcoholism, workaholism, there seems to be this "ism" hanging over our heads. We need to get to the core of this, so that we can allow that "ism" to pass through and out. That "ism" will pass through once we begin to complete our pain and grief work. It ain't easy, but it sure is worth it.

Do you want to go through life as a victim?

Me neither!!!

I want to be a survivor. A liver of life!! I want to be a vibrant part of my community. I want to live. That makes me a winner. A survivor. And it makes you a winner as well.

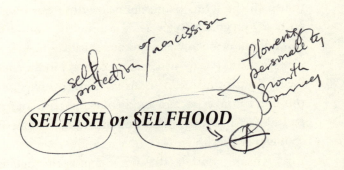

SELFISH or SELFHOOD

Hey, wait a minute, isn't there another chapter in this book on self indulgence or self nurturing? And doesn't selfish and self-indulgent mean exactly the same thing? What's going on?

Several years ago I facilitated a workshop I wrote called **"People in Transition".** While doing the research for this workshop I came across some information defining the words "selfish" and "selfhood". Did you know what these words are diametrically opposed? According to the Oxford dictionary "selfish" means "devoted to or concerned with one's own advantage or welfare to the exclusion or regard for others". "Self hood" means "the quality by virtue of which one is oneself; personal individuality; that which constitutes one's own self or individuality".

When I view "selfhood" in this context, the furthest thing from my mind is the type of selfhood that we normally think of in our western civilization. The two have no correlation at all.

I think it is really important for us as Adult Children to define these terms within our own heads. This ultimately results in the terms being defined within our own hearts, and I think, goes a long way to healing the wounds that are throughout our emotions and our spirits.

We cannot heal ourselves until we get in touch with the "self". To do this means that we have an obligation to go through the layers of ego and denial and pain and anguish, and all of the things that we have talked about in other chapters of this book.

I think another difference between "selfish" and "selfhood" really is the line of denial that we draw between these two words.

To be in "selfhood" is to be prepared to get to know our issues and to deal with them accordingly. To be "selfish" is to deny our issues and thus deny ourselves.

Each of us knows many people who fit in to the selfish category. And a lot of us know that, in our own past, we also have fit into the selfish category.

Selfish, I think, represents the person, for one reason or another, who is having trouble dealing with who he/she really is. He/she is covering up an entire mask of insecurities, so he/she puts on various acts to attain what he/she thinks he/she wants.

I have done it. You have done it. We have all done it.

Throughout my life, I have not met or seen one exception.

I also know that I will do it again, and you will do it again, but with diligence and foresight, we will do it less as time goes by.

Do what less?

Be selfish, of course.

We are a network of human beings. Each of us is alone and each of us is intrinsically linked to the other. From being alone to being intrinsically linked to others, we create the Collective Consciousness, and the Collective Consciousness rules. (Another Universal Principle).

This is all pretty basic stuff.

It is really interesting how quickly we can step aside from that and get caught up in our own self centred areas and miss the definitions of where we are meant to be.

What definitions are you talking about, you ask?

I think the definitions break down into one word – ego. If we put ego in place of self and selfish in place of selfhood, we have the two words wrapped up in pretty solid nutshells.

We are human beings with all sorts of fallibilities that wander around inside of us, and we are going to get these two definitions confused. When we are living in some sort of denial, it is easy to confuse ego and selfhood. That is what makes it an ongoing process.

One way to recognize where we are at, is if we feel stuck. Why are we stuck? What is happening in us and around us that keeps us stuck. We can feel stuck for days, weeks, years. Many things inside of us, and around us, keeps us stuck. What are we denying? Until we look at whatever that denial is, we will continue to remain stuck. When we go into our own pain, and bring it to the light, things around us begin to move. And we begin moving forward in a more healthy way. That is getting out of our selfishness and into our selfhood.

None of us can be a positive link in Humanity's tapestry unless we put selfhood first. Once we do that we cannot help but reach out to the next person or persons in this tapestry and begin the bonding mechanisms that form a healthy Collective Consciousness. We cannot have a healthy Collective Consciousness until we have healthy people. There is no escaping it.

There was a bumper sticker around some years ago that said "peace begins with me". I eventually discovered that the bumper sticker came from the Unity Church and it took me awhile to figure out what the heck it really meant. Peace was global wasn't it? What did puny me have to do with the global reality as it exists today? And tomorrow? Or over the next generation?

The more peaceful I became within different areas of my life, the more peaceful energy I emanated and the less problems I had to deal with. And when situations do arise (and, of course, they will), the Serenity Prayer is very quickly brought back into my frontal cortex, just like a mantra. This serves to remind me that I am not dealing with my "selfhood". Because, somewhere along the line, as I was dealing with a particular situation, I got into the little "i". In other words, I got into the ego.

If we have sense enough to work a Twelve Step program, one of the very first things we are going to learn is that our lives have become unmanageable and we are willing to turn our lives over to our Higher Power. If we start mucking around in the mud pies and don't allow our Higher Power to create what needs to be created, our egos are getting in the way. Our selfishness is stopping our "selves" from becoming what they truly need to be.

I learned a lot from my hairdresser. Over the years, I discovered that not only my hair was being attended to but so was my spirit. My spirit was being attended to by various people in the shop who were there, they thought, to just get their hair done. You see, the place I went to get a haircut had a clientele largely composed of people who were in recovery. A large percentage, probably about 99.9%, were heavily involved in attending to the needs of their own trilogies.

They talked about sensible diet, good exercise programs, and spiritual growth.

They talked freely about miracles.

I always came away from this person's shop knowing that miracles are far more common than we believe them to be. I came away not only feeling that my hair was being attended to, but that a piece of myself had also been put in place.

Here is an example. One day there was a woman there whom I had previously never met. She talked about how her life had taken a 360 degree turn within about three years. The previous three years she had lost her job, hit bottom, went through several personal catastrophes, realized that she had to dry out and clean up or she wasn't going to make it.

This woman looked absolutely radiant. She had a great job that she loved. She had made wonderful friends. She had a lifestyles that she only thought happened to other people.

She said "If someone were to ask me to write my own script, never in my wildest dreams would I have written a script as good as the one I am now living". She also knew that she deserved her new life and had the tools in place so she would not sabotage it. It was truly a heartwarming story.

Without know it, she has passed on to me some extremely valuable information. I was stuck. I didn't know why I was stuck, and I had been working hard to get myself unstuck, and I was not being successful. I wasn't being successful because I didn't feel worthy and I had not TURNED IT OVER. I was trying to write my own "wellness" script. When that realization came to me, it was only a matter of 48 hours when the rest fell into place. What I needed to do became apparent. I TURNED IT OVER, and I began to honour my "selfhood"). And I was looking forward to the rest of the process.

All of this information and knowledge, from that one day, taught me that knowing my "self", sure beat the recurring headaches, the lack of energy, the sugar and nicotine fixes that I had carried for so many years.

It is so very easy to slip away from selfhood and into selfishness. And it is really easy to beat ourselves up for it.

Do we need to do that? No, we do not.

We only need to TURN IT OVER.

I learned that when I really, really got in touch with that mysterious whatever that was plaguing my psyche and causing me to be selfish, that I was able to deal with the sugar and the cigarettes, and the headaches just magically disappeared.

LONELINESS or ALONENESS

Have you ever met anyone at any time in your life who did not feel acute loneliness? Sometimes the loneliness comes in waves, will stay with us for a period of time and disappear. Sometimes the loneliness is like a gnawing ache in the pit of the belly that we learn to live with on a daily basis.

Each person experiences it. Each person deals with it in a different way. It is a certainty that we all suffer from it.

I once heard loneliness described as the human condition.

Growing up in a dysfunctional environment certainly sets up a pattern of loneliness that each of us becomes extremely familiar with. And very fearful of.

Our co-dependent needs demand that we reach out of ourselves and into another sphere so that we can latch on to something or someone to assuage the pain that we are feeling somewhere deep in our souls.

Loneliness causes people to drive themselves in many directions. We can drive ourselves to great heights of achievement and we can also drive ourselves into great depths of despair. We believe that if we are accepted by someone externally and not at some basic need within ourselves we can begin to deal with this loneliness and live happily ever after.

That never happens.

When we are still in our denial systems we see loneliness as that great weapon that we need to fight at any cost so that we can find some peace of mind. And our denial system lets us do that. As we have placed that denial around us so carefully brick by painful brick, it is easier to deal with by looking for external answers for our loneliness rather than dealing with the pain of the denial.

I remember spending my fortieth birthday at the "in" supper club in the city (otherwise known as the current meat market). My friends and I had a wonderful dinner and enjoyed a couple of bottles of good wine. After dinner we wandered upstairs to see who was on the dance floor. We couldn't find a place to sit when I spotted a woman sitting alone at a table. I asked her if she would mind if we joined her. With her permission, we sat down. Within a few minutes she revealed that she had been newly separated, within the last month, was feeling terribly lonely, and had ventured out by herself into the meat market to find some company and comfort. She was terrified. The loneliness had increased to such a level in that atmosphere that she could barely deal with it.

I really related to her. I was never good at going into a meat market scene, playing a flirting game, and leaving without some scar. The whole thing seems very empty and shallow. This woman, in her high sense of need and vulnerability was in the worst place she could be, and at the worst time. And we told her that. She was looking around the room and saying "Of my God, is this all I have to look forward to?" "Is this what my life is going to be like?" "I can't stand this!"

We spent a long time with this woman, telling her that she would have been a lot better off staying at home with a book or going to a movie with a friend than coming into a nightclub where people concentrated on body images and checked their substance, and often their integrity, at the door. Eventually she felt better and was able to return home.

I have never seen that woman again, but she has left a powerful impact on my psyche.

Loneliness can really be accentuated in a crowd. Especially in a crowd of strangers.

We are all so busy wearing masks, going through the pretenses of today's civilization, concerned with the types of persona's we are presenting to the people around us that we forget to reach out and actually see, really see, what is happening in that circle.

I also remember a man speaking at one of the very first ACOA meetings about his profound sense of loneliness. He was so shaken by the loneliness that he felt, that he began to cry. The room became very still when he spoke. His pain was palpable.

We all know the loneliness of having to sit home on a Saturday night, curled up with a book or a movie, while being aware that people around us are out and busy doing things with their friends and loved ones.

I really think that loneliness is one of the biggest obstacles that we, as Recovering Co-dependents, have to overcome.

It creeps up on us in insidious ways, gnaws away at our guts and our souls, or hits us like a ton of bricks and leaves of bleeding. There doesn't seem to be any half measure with loneliness. It just niggles or whams, depending on where we are, both physically and mentally.

I think the loneliest I have ever been in my life was when I was married. Not only did my husband and I have very little in common, we also had incredible walls. Put the two together and we might as well have been sitting on opposite sides of town, rather than sitting in the same living room or, in fact, sleeping in the same bed. Neither of us had anyone to talk with. He spent more and more time with his buddies in the bar, and I spent more and more time going into deep depression.

Looking back, I realized that we were both trying to escape the loneliness each of us felt and we were doing it the only way that each of us knew how.

I don't think this is a particularly unusual story. If we were to take a poll among divorced people across North America we would discover that, among all of the fancy words placed on divorce petitions, the bottom line would probably read the same. "This relationship is terribly lonely."

So, we are fighting to stay in a relationship that is terribly lonely. Because we are still dealing with our own individual denial systems, we go into people pleasing. The more we do for the other person, the more they will respond (we hope), the more love we will have returned, the less lonely we will be, and the circle just keeps going round and round in an an ever widening pattern as it continues to grow more vicious.

Somehow we have to take that weapon of loneliness and turn it into the tool of aloneness.

For most of us it takes years. We are not taking this wall down brick by brick. We are taking this wall down inch by square inch. It is a very tedious process. I don't think we totally overcome it, either, but I do think we get a real handle on the loneliness and turn it around into the tool of aloneness.

It is extremely important for each of us to become sufficient within ourselves so that we can examine our own trilogies and see what it is within ourselves that needs to be nurtured, so we can become whole. The more whole we feel as individuals, the more the loneliness will dissipate and the aloneness will come into play. Isn't that one and the same thing, you ask? Not in the least.

Aloneness means that we are willing, and indeed happy, to have a Saturday evening at home to do exactly what it is that we need to do for ourselves. Aloneness means getting to know who we are as individuals. Aloneness is getting to know what we like to do as individuals. Aloneness is getting in touch with ourselves and becoming whole.

The great thing about this is we can be lonesome for someone, but that lonesome feeling does not interfere with our own feelings of aloneness.

How do you feel about yourself at this particular time? How do you feel about yourself when there is no-one else around except, perhaps, your favourite pet? There you are, in an old pair of slippers, or in baggy yoga pants, just being you. How do you feel? Are you comfortable with that? Why are you comfortable with that? And if you are not comfortable, why not?

It is an evolution. We have to take that evolutionary process and break it down even further. If we are in a relationship that is healthy and the other person in the relationship has gone away for a few days, we will miss him/her. However, how are we using our time? It is OK to miss the other person, that is healthy. It is also OK to take that time and feed ourselves.

Have you had the time to work your favourite cross word puzzle, read the latest book by our favourite author, take a long bubble bath, bone up on your hockey scores, watch your favourite movie, or write in your journal? When was the last time that you felt comfortable with this? Are you comfortable doing that occasionally? Are you comfortable doing that on a regular basis? Are you comfortable doing that almost every night of the week?

How much time do you spend in meditation? We have explored meditation and what it will do. Meditation is a great tool to help us deal with loneliness and get on with the business of aloneness.

We can get sabotaged on this aloneness stuff, as well. We can go along thinking that we have figured it all out, that it is working to our benefit, only to glance down and realize that we are eating our third chocolate bar, and thinking about that piece of cake sitting in the back of the fridge. If we are stuffing ourselves, there is a good chance we are stuffing our loneliness.

Time to take a look. We need to survive these emotions. For me, food had become my criteria for recognizing that I had stepped from my aloneness into my loneliness. The trick is to find whatever it is.

Differentiating between loneliness and aloneness can become such a complex challenge that we can get mired down in the dilemma of attempting to solve it. However, while we are putting new tools into our survival kit, and we become aware that we feel more comfortable within our own skins, we become more comfortable within ourselves. The more comfortable we become within ourselves, the more aloneness we can handle and we deal with loneliness in a healthier way.

My yoga teacher once said that the reason we feel loneliness is because of a primal need to connect with Universal Knowledge. I heard her say that long before I went into recovery and it has stayed with me for many years, because I have found that, ultimately, it is true. However, we can only connect to Universal Knowledge if we are in touch with ourselves.

If I don't feel at peace with myself I feel lonely. If I don't feel at peace with myself I had better find out why. I have to be at peace with myself before I can be at peace with those around me. And it is challenging.

One of the things that happens as we travel the recovery road is that the people in our lives begin to see either subtle or dramatic changes, often before we see them ourselves, and these people drift out of our sphere. Because recovery sets up vulnerability, it is really easy to take the vulnerability and turn it into loneliness. All of a sudden these people we thought of as friends, are now people that we have less in common with. We are continually adjusting our dance. While we adjust our dance, we throw our dance partners off and they lose step. And we lose step. It is easier with friends. More challenging with relations.

There is a light at the end of the tunnel. There is a Universal Truth that says that how we feel deep inside of us will be reflected on our outer reality, and other circumstances will manifest to produce for us, more fulfilling lives. That is where the circle now becomes a healing circle. It has to be within before it can be without.

If we are running around all hollow inside, looking for another influence to fill us up, we are not going to find it. At least we are not going to find it for any length of time. If we are busy filling up our own well deep inside of us by nurturing our own trilogies, we manifest that and by some form of Universal Magic what we really need just comes to us.

That doesn't sound very practical, does it? It sounds like nonsense. But it's not.

One way to test this Truth is to put yourself in a retreat. Retreats for people in recovery become fairly second nature. Of course, most of the time, when we go on a retreat, we are surrounded by other people. But the fact remains, while we are on that retreat, we are dealing with an issue that is within us. That issue can set us apart from the other people on the retreat. That retreat can have a lot of different meanings, depending on the circumstances, but either way, if it is a retreat you will benefit from, ultimately you will feel more whole.

Do I hear you say, "I've never been on a retreat, and I wouldn't know where to start to even look for one." Well, a retreat doesn't necessarily mean that you go to a monastery high on a hill, sleep on a 24 inch cot, and eat dry toast for breakfast. A retreat can mean taking cooking classes at a seaside lodge for a week-end. A retreat can mean finding a friend that you are comfortable with, hopping in a car or on an airplane and disappearing for a couple of days to somewhere quiet, or even taking a vacation by yourself. A retreat can only mean shutting your door on a Friday night, deciding that you need a week-end just for yourself, and just put-zing around doing what you want to do.

If you are finding this challenging, take out that trusted piece of paper and pencil, and write a list of all the things you would like to do over a two or three day period. Is it that cooking school, a ceramics class, a fishing trip? Is it catching up with your reading?

Make a list. Examine your list in a detached way and fit one of the items on your list around your budget and your lifestyle. And then just go and do it.

To see how you progress during your retreat, keep a journal. You don't have to write copious numbers of pages, you can just write little thoughts that pop into your head, or a paragraph at the end of the day. When you come away from your retreat, take out your journal and look back at what you wrote. I'll bet you will be surprised.

The other neat thing that happens is that you have taken a safe risk with yourself and you will feel better for having done it. You have taken a risk that says you want to get to know who you really are, and you will learn, we all learn, that we like ourselves a whole lot better than we thought we did.

As we learn this very valuable lesson we become whole. We become less lonely, more in tune with ourselves, more in tune with our Higher Power, and feel comfortable in our aloneness. And as we feel more comfortable in our aloneness, we become more whole. It creates a healing circle.

We are in a win/win situation and it feels good.

SECRECY or PRIVACY

This book has been written for people who have done some recovery work and are now in the process of trying to rebuild and rethink their behaviour patterns, simply because the old patterns we have carried around with us for so many years as Adult Children, do not work for us as adults.

However, having said that, if anyone reading this book has been hoarding a secret that needs to be told, get into a group and tell it.

If you are in a relationship that is causing you any type of mental or physical cruelty **RUN, DON'T WALK, TO THE NEAREST HELP LINE YOU CAN FIND.** This includes your relationship with yourself.

If you are not being physically or mentally abused by someone else, but feel that you are physically or mentally abusing yourself, **RUN, DON'T WALK, TO THE NEAREST HELPLINE.**

We are very fortunate to live in a society where help is a phone call away. **GET HELP IMMEDIATELY.**

Help can come to you through various anonymous groups, through a trusted minister or rabbi, through a doctor, a teacher, counselor or social workers, as well as many government agencies which have been put in place to help you protect yourself.

USE THEM – QUICKLY! BEFORE IT'S TOO LATE. THIS IS YOUR FIRST STEP ON THE ROAD TO RECOVERY.

There is a saying among people in anonymous groups that we are only as sick as our secrets. A friend and I were talking over dinner. She and I were talking about events in our lives that, at the time they were happening, made absolutely no sense. She said "you never really know about your neighbour's secrets until you walk into a meeting,." "That is where all the pieces begin to fall into place."

Secrets are seditious. We all carry them around with us in one form or another. Some are really nasty, some are overwhelming, some are downright evil. We all have them.

Some of them have left such deep emotional scars we have blocked them from our conscious minds.

We learned through recovery that, as we are ready, each secret surfaces and we are able to deal with that secret in a safe and loving environment. We are able to bring it out into the light, examine it, do our forgiveness work, and begin to put it behind us. Secrets only flourish in the dark. Once the light is shown on them they can only shrivel up into more manageable proportions. Evil doesn't like the light of day. Neither do secrets.

Our forgiveness work falls under categories of forgiving friends, acquaintances, enemies, that mugger on the street, and forgiving ourselves. It also means learning how to forgive our families of origin.

Secrecy has absolutely nothing to do with privacy. The two are so diametrically opposed that they are at opposite ends.

Because secrets can be so evil, it is not a good idea to discuss secrets with someone or in some group that is not totally safe. We need those safety nets around us to bring the secrets out. And we often need the anonymity of a safe group. We need to feel nurtured while we are doing it. Telling secrets to an acquaintance, co-worker, a relation still in denial, can and will do nothing for us. Often it will only make the secret appear more evil than it already is. It is important for us to remember that we must use good judgment and learn to reveal our secrets in an atmosphere of safety. There are no exceptions to this.

For me, the safest way to reveal my secrets was through a 12 Step Program. When we can connect the telling of our secrets with a Higher Power it goes a long way to relieving our burden of guilt.

When we need to reveal how we have harmed other people and do our amends (Steps 8 and 9) we are definitely on the first bend of the path of recovery. The burden lifted is well worth the effort. As we continue to work the 12 Steps these burdens become easier to handle and we are able to see each one with more clarity and begin to give it up. And our lives are richer for it. It now becomes imperative to us as Adult Children to deal with our secrets on an ongoing basis so that we can continue to become healthy.

Our privacy, on the other hand, needs to be protected while we are dealing with our secrets. It is neither wise nor healthy for the world to know our secrets. We need to take our privacy and handle it with care. There are few exceptions to this rule, and even those exceptions, those people who decide to break their anonymity while they are doing their 12 Step work, and beyond, know it is wise to maintain a semblance of privacy, not only for themselves, but for the people whom they hold near and dear.

Our privacy needs to be protected to help us maintain our sense of balance. Everyone has a different reality, and people will see certain disclosures that we make in a very different light than we ourselves see them. Sometimes, while we are pushing buttons, people will act defensively because we have unknowingly hit one of their secrecy buttons and they will lash out accordingly.

There are millions of people who have worked 12 Step programs, continue on with their lives, and no one knows except their sponsors and their immediate families. Millions of people continue to function in the business world and in the community at large who will not, under any circumstances, break their anonymity.

The rights of everyone need to be respected. There are no exceptions. The old saying that it takes one to know one, certainly is used here. If you have worked a 12 Step program you become familiar with the lingo. If you are working in an office environment, and you are intuitive, it doesn't take long before it becomes apparent that someone you may be working closely with is a recovering alcoholic, for instance. Remarks will be made. Remarks like "I take it one day at a time", "When I drank", "easy does it". Remarks that only the initiated will pick up on. Only the initiated will pick up on it, and only the initiated will honour it. That person has not come out and said "I am a recovering alcoholic." "I am an Adult Child." "I am a Co-dependent." "I am a recovering addict."

When we are in recovery ourselves, the last thing we would do is pry for information. That person has the right to protect his/her privacy. Indeed, his/her livelihood may depend on it. No one has the right to pry into his/her personal affairs.

In the broader spectrum, a great many employers now offer Employee Assistance Programs (EAP) for employees who need help. That privacy must never be broken. The code of silence around someone's recovery must remain intact. The employer has set up a win/win situation. By honouring the employee's privacy, the employer is going to get a better employee, a better person, a better worker, a better contributor to the whole.

When you think of privacy through every day living, each of us meets hundreds of people in the course of our lives who we would not want to know where we lived. We don't want these people to know our address for a variety of reasons – and this can vary from the area of town that we live in, the environment that we are surrounded by, or because we don't want to be bothered.

Almost everyone has some notoriety within his/her community. An athlete, a politician or celebrity, does not publish his/her telephone number. More often than not, if you wanted to contact one of these people you could probably do it through your computer, but you would also probably have a tough time finding out where they lived. And that is as it should be. These people are putting a lot on the line every day of their lives. We all need a place where we can come to, relax, and feel safe. Somewhere we can go and and lounge around in those yoga pants and just be ourselves. No fanfare, no show of hands, no criticisms, no adulation, just peace and quiet.

We need to surround ourselves with that type of privacy to allow ourselves to grow. The privacy helps us to nurture our aloneness. Our aloneness helps us to nurture our connection with our own Higher Power.

One of the places it is difficult to maintain any physical or emotional privacy is, often, within the confines of a family unit. A family unit still living in denial can seem to take a great deal of vicarious delight in trying to pry information from other members of the family. Sometimes a family member simply is not ready or willing to share information. Sometimes the member of that family needs time to think through an issue that he/she is working with. Sometimes that member is battling the vices of his/her own secrets. Whatever the reasons, we need to respect that need to privacy. If we really love someone in the true sense of the word "love", we will not pry.

We will honour that person enough to respect their boundaries, and feel secure enough within ourselves to know that when that person is ready to confront an issue, he/she will make that phone call or appear at our door.

I personally have found this difficult, because I am a mother of two grown daughters. When one of my daughters is hurting it is all I can do to hold myself back and keep my emotional distance. I can put such tight reigns on myself that I can be accused of being aloof when the fact is that initially my intentions were good and I wanted to give them their own space to deal with their own issues. It's important that we learn that the balance of giving space must equal the balance of reaching our a helping hand. If the hand is slapped away, there is little else any of us can do but kiss the hand better and wait it out. The only exception I know of is when a loved one is being physically abused, refuses to acknowledge that abuse, and we continue to do nothing. That is one time that we must act.

For the most part, we must recognize that each of us is on our own journey. Each of us must make our own mistakes and create our own realities. My journey is not the journey of my daughters. My journey is not the journey of my friends. My journey is not the journey of any of my relations. My journey is mine. Their journey is theirs. And privacy is established.

If someone tells us that its none of our business, it is best to take that statement at face value. For whatever reason that person has, he/she feels very strongly that it is none of our business and we need to honour that.

In large families, physical privacy can be an extremely difficult thing to achieve. All the rooms in the house are full. People are going about their business. The television is blaring. The computer is on. Snacks are being brought out of the fridge. People are constantly stumbling over each other.

If we are in that type of an environment find somewhere that you can go where you can build up your sense of privacy. Very often it may not be in your own home, but then again, maybe it will. How many times have you visited a friend only to discover that right next to the John there is a well stocked magazine rack? One of the best places in the house to have some privacy is the bathroom. There may be screams from the other side of the door but you are guaranteed a few minutes by yourself. And sometimes that is all it takes.

When I was a kid growing up, the most private place I had was the movie house. I saw three movies a week. Every time I got money, my family knew there was one place they could find me and that was at the movies. Another thing that worked for me was swimming. Swimming can be an isolating sport. I could go to the pool and do fifty laps and not have one soul bother me. Not only was I exercising my body, I was also exercising my right to privacy. And I still swim.

If you live in a situation where privacy is difficult to achieve, spend some time checking out your options, and then act on them. It will only be a matter of time before you come up with a game plan for yourself to allow yourself the privacy that you need to maintain your own sense of equilibrium. As you begin to honour your need for privacy, you will begin to honour the need for privacy in people around you.

Everything seems to work that way, doesn't it? The more we honour our own needs, the more we honour the needs of others.

IN THE STARS? or IN ME?

[handwritten annotations: "zodiac -'fate'" vs "choice/self actualization"]

From a modern point of view, it probably started back in the sixties – when today's yuppies were yesterday's hippies, wandering around and saying "peace, brother" and heavily involved in breaking colour barriers and stopping a war. That may have been when the pick-up line started which goes like this: "What is your sign?"

One of the things that is discussed among people, either seriously or as a form of entertainment, and within the confines of metaphysics, as well, is the twelve signs of the Zodiac.

For instance, I know that I am an Aquarius, and that this is the eleventh sign of the Zodiac, and that makes me a water bearer, and that also makes me altruistic and would like to leave the world a better place than when I got here this time round. I have also read that I can be moody and irascible and that I am very loyal to family and friends.

I doubt there is a newspaper on the North American Continent that does not supply each reader with his/her daily horoscope. I also doubt that most people read it, for one reason or another, be it for face value or for entertainment. Or possibly, somewhere in between.

I don't know very much about this subject. But one thing I do know is that very often, for reasons that escape me, someone can tell personality traits of another person by virtue of what sign they were born under and where their ascendancies are. I'm still not sure what "ascendancies" mean, but they are in there somewhere. I find the business of astrology really fascinating. I mean, how did people come up with this stuff?

Several years ago I had a friend whose whole life was given over to scientific pursuits. The man was brilliant. He had an IQ that was somewhere in the stratosphere. He had several degrees, and his attitude was one of intense curiosity with an "I'll believe you, but prove it". He was so intelligent that he found it painful to be around most people because they bored him silly. Consequently, he spent a great deal of time alone, and he might correct me on this, but I think he became his own best friend. Which ain't bad.

He arrived in town, unexpectedly, and phoned to ask if I wanted to have dinner with him. I had made a previous engagement with another woman friend of mine and asked him if he would like to join us. He said he was delighted, and the three of us proceeded to go out for Chinese food. The woman friend was the total opposite of my scientific friend. Her personality can best be described as that of an Auntie

Mame. She had legions of friends and acquaintances, was always throwing parties, wore off-the-wall clothes extremely well, and was the only person I knew who could decorate her condo in dark greens and purples and have it look smashing. She generally appeared to walk through life on a cloud. She was great fun. So, my scientific friend and my Auntie Mame friend had never met, nor had I ever discussed either of them with the other. My scientific friend, within a very short time, was beginning to show signs of agitation because of this lady who kept coming out with outrageous statements that she could not back up. Furthermore, he had been traveling a great deal, was tired, and generally felt quite put upon. "Mame", in her intuitive way, picked up on this. She asked my friend what sign he was born under and proceeded to tell him that she thought it was probably Virgo. He looked at her in surprise, and then at me for confirmation. I told him that she would have no way of knowing.

For the next half hour, she sat across the table from him and told him about parts of his personality that only he would know, or perhaps someone who knew him very well may have an inkling about, because this man was very private.

I don't know how she did it. She did it, she said, because my friend was a Virgo. She said that all the information she needed to know about his personality, was there before her and she fed these parts to him, one at a time, like a long line of treats. My scientific friend was amazed and somewhat uncomfortable.

Astrology may be a complex, and sometimes helpful, way of analyzing our own lives. But, in the final analysis, I think, it is still up to each individual.

It is so easy to put the blame on something else if we don't want to look at our own issues.

I knew a woman who brought her Astrological chart to work at the beginning of each month. You know, one of those charts you can buy in any drugstore or supermarket. Each morning, when she came to work, it was the very first thing she looked at. And from that chart she decided how her day was going to be. If there was a "warning" on that chart she would look it over and say "well, it's going to be one of those days". And, you know, she was right. If it said she was going to be her lucky day for the month, she would immediately break into a big smile and say "isn't that great?" "It is going to be a great day!" And she was usually right. She had herself so programmed by reading this little chart from the drugstore that, for awhile, they really worked for her. I remember suggesting that she do it backwards. In other words, do it at the end of each day to see how it fit. She said "no", she preferred to be warned.

Well, I ran that experiment on myself, as I'm sure a lot of people have also done. I read my horoscope at the end of each day to see how well it fit, and 99 times out of 100 it had absolutely nothing to do with things that had transpired that day. I just chalked it up to its entertainment value.

I do believe, however, that certain parts of us are affected by the full moon, because of the water tables within our bodies. Statistics also tell us that more babies are born, there are more accidents, crime rates increase, and people seem to be a lot more edgy. Often, as I go about my daily business, I'll ask myself if it's a full moon because of different actions and reactions going on around me, and more often than not, it will be a full moon or a new moon. One way or another the moon seems to affect people's water tables and they act or react accordingly.

How often do we hear someone say "I can't help doing what I am doing, or being what I am being because I am a Taurus, a Leo, a Cancerian", etc. Geminis are great for this because they are the twins of the Zodiac and, as such, are supposed to have double personalities. And there seems to be some truth to that. I often hear Geminis say "I just can't help myself – it is the Gemini in me".

I think this is a real cop out. This means that our denial systems are so entrenched that there is absolutely no way that we can deal with any of our own pain issues, so we have to blame our behavior on something. What better thing to blame them on than our birth sign? God knows, we can't blame it on our parents or any of our primary caregivers. Because, if we do that we are liable to let the cat out of the bag. So, the thing we do is blame our birth sign again. We just keep blaming. Because, for awhile, that is just easier.

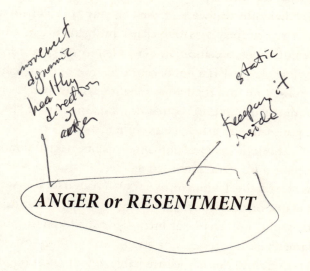

ANGER or RESENTMENT

Anger is good. Anger is healthy.
Anger needs to be dealt with. One of the areas we really get into trouble with is walking around being angry for a lot of our lives and not knowing why. That burning anger turns to deep resentment. The resentment then manifests itself in all sorts of different ways. It can manifest as depression. Anger turned inward is depression. It can manifest as headaches, ulcers, colitis. Different types of diseases will have their root in anger. Psychologically, we can deal with our resentments in an unhealthy way by acting out unmet developmental needs. Our resentments then manifest in unhealthy rages and we lash out at all of the wrong people and usually at all of the wrong times.

It is really important that we define our anger.

Once we have dealt with our core issues and we are now getting on with our lives, and something happens today that makes us really angry, we can take a look at what this is. If you are having trouble deciding where that anger is coming from because you are living within the emotion of anger itself, it is a good idea to just start writing things down. Write things down as they come to you. Is the anger coming from a specific person or event, something you have no control over? Where is it coming from?

Once you have taken a look at where your anger is coming from your anger is a whole lot easier to deal with. This is what we want to do. We want to deal with that anger in as healthy a manner as we know how. We do not want to sidestep it. We can't go around it, we have to go through it. If the anger is directed at a specific person, we can do one of two things. We can either address the person to get the anger out; or, if that's not possible because of distance or circumstances, or whatever, then we have to deal with it in a different way. But, if we want to deal with our anger directly with the person involved, then we have to take a look at it from the first person point of view.

Because truth can often be very subjective, and the other person's truth may not necessarily be your truth, whatever has happened to make you angry, the other person may not realize that he/she, in turn, has made you angry. When we come to deal with this, it is really important that we deal with it on a first person basis. In other words, we say to that person "I am really angry. I am angry at this specific behavior". Because, the words and the behavior are what we are angry with, and not the person.

It is really important to remember that people are pressing our own buttons, and we are getting angry at very specific reasons that are, more often than not, deeply imbedded within our own subconscious.

We need the tools to deal with this anger. If we can't reach that person and deal with the anger on a first person basis, we need other tools. We can take a long walk. We can practice Yoga. We can involve ourselves in a favourite sport. We can go golfing and put that person's head on the golf ball and just keep whacking it off for all eighteen holes. Whatever it takes it is imperative we get the heat out of our anger. As long as that anger sits in there we are going to keep it, not only in our subconscious level, but it will also manifest in our bodies. It is imperative we learn how to deal with it.

When we have a full tool chest, it makes it much easier for us to go into that tool chest and pick out the appropriate tool. Like a specific anger at a specific time. One theory is that at the root of all anger is fear.

When I look back over most of the stuff that I got and still get angry with, I can usually put fear in there. Fear of abandonment, fear of invalidation, are all fears that need to be addressed. However, it is almost impossible to address these basic fears until we address the anger itself.

Haven't you ever found yourself in a situation where something has happened or someone has done you a disservice and you have looked at someone else and said "I don't understand why that happened, but I am certainly not angry about it".

Of course you are angry!!

You would not be human if you weren't angry!

The difference between trying to explain your anger away and looking at your anger, is fear of your anger. And your anger simply must be expressed. Somehow it needs to come out. And in a healthy manner. Healthy for you, and healthy for those around you.

People who do cruel and inhuman things to others, places and events are doing so, I think, because they don't know how to deal with their anger. They are reacting to the negativity around them in the only way that their psyche's know. And that is the danger.

Many of the problems that we are facing in our society are coming from fear and anger. People do commit murders and travesties. Man's inhumanity to man is an unholy means for people to act out of deep seated anger and fear that they don't know how to handle.

Can we overcome it? Yes we can. How? Group support. Hard work? The hardest. Worth it? You bet!!

BEING IN CONTROL or BEING ALL TOGETHER

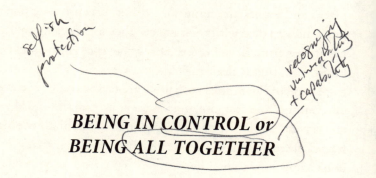

Robin Norwood, in her book, "Women who Love Too Much", says that "Denial feeds the need to control, and the inevitable failure to control feeds the need to deny".

While we are going through our own recovery process, we discover that there are as many areas of control as there are stars in the sky. We just never think of it in those terms.

Most of us think of control as something or someone who is autocratic in his/her behaviour, or a system that is really hard line.

For me, control always meant "synonymous with being under someone's thumb". It never occurred to me that there were any other types of control. And it certainly never occurred to me that I was a person who had any type of control issues myself. Heaven forbid. Only people I was mad at seemed to need to control, and gosh, I was never mad at myself, and even if I ever was mad at myself, why would I need control?

Was I wrong!!

And if felt good to be wrong. I learned a lot about myself but I also learned how necessary it was to begin to heal a lot of this stuff, to see it for what it was and to begin the healing process. I also learned to see subtle control issues from other people. These control issues come from all sorts of interesting places.

One of the places that control manifests is with people who create chaos. If you don't want to attend to stuff that is going on in your life, and you don't want to have to take a look at any of your own issues, it is really easy to keep yourself in a chaotic form of living. Because, if you are keeping yourself in a state of chaos, you have absolutely no time to take a look at the reasons why you are in this chaos. That feels, somehow, very comfortable. The reason this feels comfortable is that is what we learned at the feet of our primary caregivers who raised us in chaotic households. We tend to carry with us what we feel the most comfortable with, and chaos is one of them. Chaos is also a means of control. And that is the dichotomy, if ever there was one, but it really does exist.

Let's look at an example. If you know someone who you are not paying too much attention, as far as he/she is concerned, that person could set herself/himself up in all sorts of way to get your attention. One way is by making sure that everything around him/her is in total chaos. Someone is going to have to step in and try to help sort through the chaos. Right? Right. So, there you are and here is this person. Mother. Father. Uncle. Aunt. Sibling. Husband. Wife. Child. He/she is creating an incredible amount of chaos. He/she can't hold a job. He/she can't control his/her finances. He/she has relatives and friends calling constantly and they all want something. A lot of people that he/she knows or in his/her family, have drinking and/or drug problems. There are a lot of "isms" floating around him/her all over the place. He/she is accident prone. His/her personal habits are usually below standard, and by that I mean that the toilet bowl hasn't been washed out for months and you can hardly stand to use the biffy. That is just something that never occurs to him/her. You are damn lucky if you even get toilet paper. This is chaos. And it sounds opposite to the persnickety person who has to have everything perfect at any cost, doesn't it? It is not.

We all know someone who creates chaos at work. You know the type of person. He/she is always disorganized. It doesn't matter what he/she is trying to achieve, he/she is too late in achieving it. He/she cannot keep to a schedule, leaves people waiting, would take the booby prize for communication skills, so no one ever gets proper instruction. He/she just creates chaos everywhere. And you know? Everybody notices him/her. Without exception — everybody notices.

Perhaps psychologists will disagree, but I really think that is what chaos is all about. If he/she can create that type of chaos and be noticed, then he/she does not have to deal with the issues that he/she really needs to be dealing with.

I haven't seen it exactly expressed that way by any expert I have studied, but for now, I am sticking with my hypothesis.

Another thing I have noticed with this type of chaotic behaviour in the workplace is that if a man is behaving in a chaotic manner, most people around him will make comments about how busy he is, or will say that support staff will have to do what they can to cover his ass. If it is a woman who is creating this type of chaos in a working environment, more often than not, her job is in jeopardy. Whoever said that the gender issues are fair. And again, this is just an observation I've made over the years.

Eventually these people end up with two options. They either have to smarten up or self-destruct. Can any of us see ourselves in either of these two scenarios? I don't know about you, but I certainly can.

It took me years and years to understand why I had the reputation of being able to work with difficult people, because my life had already been chaotic right from the time I can remember until I worked a Twelve Step Program. I'd had a lot of different jobs, an unsuccessful marriage. I was a single parent and had several co-dependent relationships that came to hurtful endings. Chaos was my middle name. That being the case, why did I have this reputation of being able to work with difficult people?

As I worked through my own recovery it became clear one of the reasons was because I was so good at creating chaos that I was able to spot it in somebody else. The other thing I discovered was that if I was on real solid ground about the type of work I was doing, in other words if I really knew my stuff, or I knew where I could lay my hands on my stuff so that I could get that paper shuffled from the left side of my desk to the right, then I could take that chaotic behaviour on principle and place it in a detached place, and deal with the person accordingly. In other words, I knew where they were coming from. I wasn't fooled. If they wanted to go around doing all the things they did, and I was doing a good job regardless of what they were pulling off, or attempting to pull off, I had it made. Again, this only worked if I really, really knew what I was doing. I am no rocket scientist. If I were working in a lab doing rocket science work, I would fall flat on my face, no doubt about it. It was just a matter of knowing where my own boundaries lay. And that is another chapter.

You see, these difficult people were coming from the same place I was. They were just using different tactics.

We can take parts of our lives and keep those parts in total chaos so that we don't have to attend to what needs to be attended. We do this by continually acting out something that is an unmet developmental need from our early childhood. Often, we don't even realize what we are doing. We just keep doing it and don't know why our lives are in such a mess. How often have you heard yourself say "How did I get myself into this?".

Well, we got ourselves into this by not looking backwards, examining what we needed to examine, going through our grief work, and getting on with our lives.

One Day at a Time.

So, here we are, trying to control the people around us by creating our own form of chaos. Because we haven't done the work.

Most of us are familiar with control, especially with the very blatant way of controlling. The autocratic parent, etc. This one is really, really easy to spot, and most of us have had something like this in our lives at one time or another.

"There is only one way to do this, and that is my way." "Your way does not count." "It is totally wrong anyway, so it is going to be my way." "So there."

Sometimes these people get fantastic results for a short period of time, while those around them draw in their breath.

Eventually, though, these people fall over. Like everything in life, it creates a domino effect.

We also can have control issues around things like illness.

How many people have you met in your life, or perhaps you have had a mother, father or grandparent who was constantly ill.

My paternal grandfather was constantly ill. I don't think the man drew a well breath from the time I can remember until the day he died. (He proved himself right). Most of the time he really was genuinely ill. My grandfather never thought for one moment that he was faking it. But when he got really, really upset, or couldn't handle a situation that was happening in his life, he got sick.

I learned a lot about illness from my grandfather. I learned as a child that this trick really worked. I remember as a young child pulling this sick stuff, while healthy, a few times, because I knew that I would get attention, and it worked.

When I reached adulthood, I became more and more ill. Only now, I wasn't faking it. It was really there. The psyche had definitely tripped in the way I had programmed it, and I was going to be ill. I was going to prove myself right by staying in control, and I was going to be ill and I was going to get that attention. So there I was. I had created exactly what I wanted. Was it ever a mess.

Metaphysical teachers will tell you that all illness is self imposed. I don't necessarily agree that all illness is self imposed. But I do know that my childhood tapes certainly imposed a lot of my own illnesses.

The medical profession will tell you that over 90% of today's illnesses are related to stress. That seems to be true. Heart attacks can be brought on by stress. There are other causes, of course. But stress is high on the list. If we are living with a chronic condition, that condition is often exacerbated by stress.

When I began studying the impact of stress on the body, I learned that stress leaves marks on our physiology as well as our psyche's.

The stress has to come out somewhere doesn't it?

I used to hypothesize that cancer came out because of unexpressed rage. Then I got breast cancer and discovered that this particular cancer came from hormone replacement therapy. At this writing I am six years cancer free.

Stress is insidious.

In today's toxic wasteland, known as Planet Earth, (will She ever forgive us for living in chaos?) I doubt that 1/10th of 1% of the population can say that they have spent their entire lives not being sick with something.

We are all going to get the cold or flu, or some type of low grade infection, or suffer from headaches. Parts of our bodies that relate to what we do for a living will eventually manifest with a related illness or discomfort.

There are certainly mechanisms within our own trilogies that say "If your Ego won't listen to your Inner Self, then it is time I (Inner Self) took over, so you are going to get sick for a couple of days or a couple of weeks, so you can get in touch with whatever you need to get in touch with".

This is different than using illness as a control mechanism to manipulate the people around us.

We women are particularly good (bad?) at trying to control through manipulation. I don't necessarily think this is the fault of any one of us. Louise Hay, in her book "You Can Heal Your Life", says that we are all victims of victims. Lots of psychologists say that as well.

Our cultures have dictated for many centuries that women are second class citizens and don't hold a lot of worth and are not given a lot of credence. Many of us learned to get what we needed and/or wanted by manipulating the male. We also learned to manipulate other women. We had been taught early on that women needed to compete with other women. And to get what we wanted, we normally had to get a man to do that, and we were in direct competition with our neighbor next door. So the story goes.

We keep piling manipulation on top of all of the other baggage we learned in a dysfunctional home, and it spells control.

People will fight for what they believe is right at any cost. Doesn't matter. They are right. It is difficult to break that cycle. And, often, people around them just give up. And then what? Apathy.

Sounds a lot like Society in general, doesn't it?

Well, apathy is a form of control.

There is a great deal of difference between caring and not having to care. I can say "I don't care", or I can say "I don't have to care". If I don't care about something, I am apathetic. If I don't have to care about something, it leaves me "carefree".

If someone comes up to me and says "what do you think about such-and-such" and "such-and-such is being cared for appropriately, then I can honestly say "I don't care". Because it is none of my business and I do not need to have any control in that situation. It is legitimately someone else's sandbox.

If you don't give a flying damn about what is going on around you; if you hear no evil, see no evil, speak no evil, if you refuse to acknowledge that there is a problem in any area, then it really is necessary to ask yourself, are you part of the problem or part of the solution?

This sounds easy, but it is not.

It is a lot easier to spot control issues in someone else than it is in ourselves.

What are we going to do with it? You know the first thing we do with it? We give it Up.

We give it Up by admitting to ourselves, the First Step of the Twelve Steps – that our lives have become unmanageable.

This is the beginning of reclaiming our lives.

Our lives have become unmanageable because of control issues. Either our own or someone else's – and often it is a combination of both.

When we stand back and take a look, we discover that our control issues are bouncing off of somebody else's control issues, are bouncing off of somebody else's control issues, are bouncing off somebody else's control issues. And so it goes.

When we are tired of playing in this sandbox, we say "I don't want to play". We can now do our Step One work. And two or three things begin to happen.

After we recover from the shock of figuring out we are not as smart as we thought we were, and are willing to get Step 1 on paper and then talk to a sponsor, the usual emotion is a feeling of great vulnerability.

Vulnerability is good. It is needed, necessary, healthy. Vulnerability also needs to be protected.

While in this vulnerable state, we can protect ourselves by surrounding ourselves with a good support group.

It is no accident that 12 Step work is done within the confines of a group environment.

Our vulnerability is now protected by the group through the group's validation. We can feel safe within our vulnerability because the group validates us and our issues. The group says "hey, that's OK." "I know where you are coming from." "I've been there." There is no judgment.

We are no longer alone. When we are no longer alone we can be vulnerable.

OK. Now the group is validating us. What about the people within our individual life styles?

That is a totally different ball game.

Often, it is necessary to just walk away and say "no, I don't want to play anymore." "I resign from this way of doing things." This can really knock people flat on their butts; and they will react in several ways.

Sometimes they react by being defensive. Sometimes people react by being really offensive.

Eventually, though, these people will disappear from our lives. The more these people disappear from our lives, the more all-together we feel, and the better and smoother our lives begin to feel.

And this is all because we are learning how to give up control.

Being all-together, through non-control – right?

In the final analysis, what does having it all-together really mean?

To me, having it all-together means that we look after all of the parts of our trilogy, on a simultaneous basis, as best we know how.

Our trilogy is made up of three parts. Body. Mind. Spiritual Growth, which also includes Emotions.

The body is looked after by proper maintenance. We don't eat too much or too little. We don't drink. We don't smoke too much, and preferably not at all. We know how to exercise the body too much or too little. We treat the body the way it was meant to be treated. As a finely tuned mechanism that deserves our tender, loving care. The body is our vehicle to carry us through life, and it will do so admirably if we just keep it's oil changed as frequently as we do our cars.

Most of us look after our cars better than we look after our bodies. If our cars sputter, refuse to start, or the engine light comes on, we take our car to the shop and then usually take it out for a bit of a run to see how it is performing. Most of us don't think about taking our bodies out for a run; and, indeed, maybe that isn't the way to do it. Maybe we need to do some other form of cardiovascular work, like go for a healthy swim or hike, or do low impact aerobics, or yoga.

We will receive from our minds exactly what we put into them. Our mind is as precious as our body. In fact, the mind runs the body. So, it stands to reason that what we put into our mind is what we will get out of it.

How often do we think of that when we turn on the TV? When we are leafing through magazines? Wandering around the Internet? Stopping to pick up a book? See a movie? How often do we think about what we are feeding our minds?

Comic books, humorous literature, adventure stories are all good stuff when kept in the right perspective. We need to feed our minds really good food, just like we feed our bodies (hopefully).

If we fill our minds with violent thoughts, violent and angry videos, violent and angry newspapers, periodicals, books, internet "junk" (lots of it out there), that is what we are going to get back – more violence and anger. We need to feed our thoughts gently and with stretch. Then we are feeding the mind.

It is absolutely necessary that we continue to learn. We need to learn on a daily basis. To have a day without learning is to have a day without growth. We don't need to decide how to crack the atom, if we in fact have no interest in knowing that. We may decide that it would be important for us to take a pottery class and learn something that is aesthetically pleasing to us. We may decide to take night classes to upgrade our working skills. Or, we may decide to take a creative writing class, or take up golf or tennis. We may decide to join a debating team, or do the crossword puzzle in our daily newspaper. Whatever it is, on a daily basis, we need to feed our mind and learn something. Sometimes it is even necessary to get away from the day to day news. All of the violence, death, destruction and plundering plays on the subconscious and if we need to take a break from it for awhile, that's OK. Most of the stuff we see and hear are stuff we can't control, so it is absolutely OK to take a break. And like everything else, we do all this One Day at a Time.

If you do decide to become a rocket scientist it is imperative to remember the One Day at a Time rule. Remember buying a text book and flipping to the last chapter? It was all Greek. If you started on page 1 of chapter 1 it made a little more sense. Continue to learn that way. Doesn't matter what it is we are undertaking. Start at the beginning and take it One Day at a Time.

To learn is to stretch. Our mind is a muscle. It needs to have a work out. It needs to be fed, exercised and relaxed like every other part of our bodies.

How do we feed our Spirit?

Well, if we have done any 12 Step work, whether we know it or not, we are well and truly in touch with feeding the spiritual part of our lives.

A lot of people equate spirit with religion. Personally, I don't find any correlation between the two. Arnold Patent said that religion was a way to create God in man's image. For me, that sums it up.

Spirituality is that special something that is within each of us that connects with the Something that is out there, that Something that keeps us whole. It gives us hope. It gives us gentleness. It gives us laughter. It gives us caring. It gives us courage. It gives us kindness. It gives us peace. That little magic Something that is deep within each of us, that is connected with Something out there is the sum total of our spiritual development. It is our Higher Power – however we choose to acknowledge It.

And again, we feed our spiritual development the same way that we feed our body and mind, with gentle discipline and love, and

One Day at a Time.

The most important tool I have for feeding my spiritual development is through meditation. Things have a habit of running away from me if I don't meditate every day.

Everyone has a different way of getting in touch with his/her spirituality (Higher Power). For some, it is a walk in the country. For someone else it is watching a sunset. For another person it is talking with a good and trusted friend. For others it encompasses all of these things and more. When we stay disciplined about our spirituality, the growth seems to look after itself.

There you have it.

Mind, Body, Spirit, working together.

And why are they working together? Because we are feeding all at different times, with different foods and at different paces, and they come together, all by themselves.

It has nothing to do with control. Indeed, the very opposite. This is, of course, a daily monitoring. And because we never recover, we are always going to have issues, every day of our lives.

The trick is to be able to recognize those issues more easily, so we can deal with them immediately, if possible, then let them go, and keep moving forward.

CONTROLLING MY LIFE
or LIVING MY LIFE

Here are some other ways of focusing on our control issues.

There are areas of profound differences between controlling our lives and living our lives. While we are in our denial systems, we want to be in control at all costs.

We go to great lengths to achieve this. It is extremely important to control ourselves and how we act, but to control those people around us, as well. We try and have people conform to our standards of behaviour and our ways of thinking. How many women have you known throughout the years who have said, and this is particularly true of my generation, "once we get married, I will change him". It doesn't work.

We control our children with very rigid behaviour patterns.

If we are a boss, we will try and control our employees by not only having them work specific hours and on certain machinery, but we will make up all sorts of autocratic machinations to say that we are right in doing this.

On the other side of that coin, employees will look for rigid types of environments because that control helps them to define their own parameters. They just feel more safe.

We use our control issues on our exercise habits You know, has it become a compulsion, or do we exercise to keep our bodies sound?

How little or how much do we eat?

We try to control our environment as much as possible. Some people are so good at control that they end up controlling entire countries and alter the course of history for all time.

As long as our denial systems are in place, we will go to any lengths to achieve anything we think we need to do. All in the name of control.

A woman, for instance, will take compulsive pains to keep her home incredibly clean. A man will take those same compulsive pains to keep his car totally spotless.

No one is going to look under the bed that often to see if there is the odd dust bunny under there, nor is anyone going to look at the tire treads on someone's car to see if it has been properly washed, scrubbed, polished, for six hours on a sunny Saturday afternoon. Nobody cares. Except for the people doing it.

As dysfunctional people living in our denial systems, and using these methods to help us control our way of living, we are definitely going down another unhealthy path.

The trick, then, becomes one of taking all of these unhealthy outlets and doing our pain work and our recovery work to change them into healthy outlets. Then, as we get into recovery, we learn about healthy outlets and we get our lives and ourselves together. What a difference.

When we are first in recovery, we don't notice a lot of things that are happening to us. We don't notice that the odd dust ball is forming behind the bed. We don't notice that Jane Smith has put forth a political view that we don't agree with and we haven't jumped down her throat. We don't notice that John Doe has been arriving late at work every morning for the last week. And we haven't noticed because it doesn't affect us, one way or the other. It is none of our business.

We do, however, start to notice that in our own physical bodies, our muscles are not as tense as they once were. Perhaps headaches aren't quite as severe. Our shoulders are not so close to our ears. We laugh easier. We don't feel as angry all the time. We are probably sleeping better.

These are things that happen on a subtle level and over a period of time. We didn't get sick overnight and we are not going to get well overnight. So, these things can be so subtle and happen so gradually that they don't jump out at us. All of a sudden, one day, we just notice that something is there.

This is not to say that things stop going wrong in our lives. That is Life's Lesson.

How we handle those things is how we deal with those Lessons. Are we more inclined to spend some time with a close friend, or go home and do the laundry? Are we more inclined to fight for what we believe at any cost or do we listen to the other person's point of view? Maybe, just maybe, that person may have something that's worthwhile listening to. What is their truth? What is their reality?

Someone in recovery once said that she measures her own recovery in terms of the 12 Steps being a clock. She said that she finds that her recovery goes from Step 1 To Step 12 on a constant basis. She knows that when she is at the "Twelve Step Phase", 12 o'clock, on her journey that something is going to happen that is going to put her back to Step 1, where she will have to say to herself and to her Higher Power "I admitted I was powerless and that my life and become unmanageable". In other words, she turned it over to her Higher Power.

This woman also told us that every time this happens, she automatically sets herself up to go into Step 2, Step 3, Step 4, Step 5, all the way through to Step 12, again.

She told us that she does this with every specific issue that arises. This way, she keeps herself all together and out of her own control issues. She finds that, by working the 12 Steps on her own personal principles, she is able to monitor her life on a daily basis, and life runs a whole lot better.

She consistently learns when she must respond and when she must withdraw. It also keeps her in daily contact with her Higher Power. And she knows she never has to solve any problem all by herself.

She is a very serene woman and a pleasure to be with.

Her work is now going along at a higher level of consciousness than it was, and certainly when she was drinking, approximately 25 years ago.

I have used this woman's example many times in my own life. When other people's control issues confront me, I quickly reach back into my friend's life for reference and immediately place myself onto Step 1.

It works.

We have to take our control issues and deal with them on a very personal level. We can only take a look at our own life and our own behaviour patterns. Then we have to give it up. With a Capital U. On a daily basis, on an hourly basis, minute by minute, if necessary, whatever it takes. We have to give up that control.

We continue to stand up for what we believe in, and continue to be counted. We learn that we only have today and that we can only do the best that we can do with the tools that we have been given, just for today.

Tomorrow isn't here yet.

We are going to take today's tools and we are going to work in our own garden. That is all we can do. We are not expected to do anything else. We are only expected to clean up our own acts.

The ramifications of cleaning up our own acts are mighty, indeed.

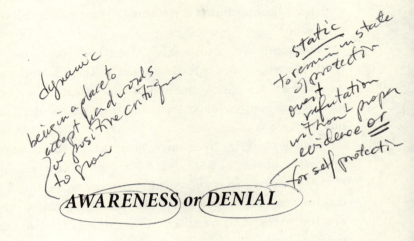

AWARENESS or DENIAL

This awareness/denial stuff can be a tough one to crack. We fluctuate back and forth on a daily basis, often slipping from one to the other without realizing that is what we are doing. Often there is such a fine line between the two that it is almost impossible, it seems, to detect where one drops off and the other one picks up.

Adult Children, I think, vacillate very easily between awareness and denial. As Adult Children we continue to act out our feelings. Feelings that were not met through our childhood and adolescence. We do this through the types of partners we choose, friends we have and situations we get ourselves into.

Most of us develop a keen intuitive sense that triggers in to our survival mechanisms when we are looking for signs of displeasure in another person. That intuitive sense, linked with our co-dependency, leads us directly down the the path of people-pleasing and that is where it becomes difficult to define the lines.

Everybody wants to be liked. Everybody needs to be liked. Everybody needs to be validated. There is nothing new in that. The trick is to be liked and validated for who we are and what we stand for rather than for our need to please someone else.

People-pleasing takes on a great many forms and, besides the obvious, we are all familiar with falling into the trap of pleasing mates and partners because we need to be daddy's little girl or mommy's little boy. We all know that one really well. And we all know that this leads to a road going nowhere.

Denial systems will trigger all other aspects of our lives, as well, in covert ways that we remain unaware of for long periods of time.

Have you ever worked in an environment where there has been someone within your working radius who you and the rest of your co-workers call an "apple polisher"? An apple polisher will jump hoops, shine shoes and pant at the prospect of pleasing a superior, and it all comes out very phoney.

To the person who is polishing the apply, it is not the least bit phoney. That person, in his own insecurity, is desperately looking for a way to receive validation and will continue to polish that apple until he finds that validation.

Unfortunately, because he is not coming from a true sense of selfhood, the result is inevitable. That is, he will end up falling flat on his face. There can be no other ending to the story. That person is so busy polishing the apple, trying to please a superior or other people around him, that he fails to meet his own needs. By failing himself he can only fail those around him, as well.

We women really fall into this denial pattern very easily. We have all been there. How does he like my hair? What is his favourite colour? What are his favourite dishes? I'd better make sure my cell phone is turned on at all times. What if he calls when I turn it off? The litany is never ending. And it goes beyond the bounds of compromise. This is discussed further in another chapter on relationships.

While we are caught up in all of these acting-out scenarios we are living in our denial systems. We continue to live in our denial when we meet someone who we find fascinating or intriguing, decide to get to know them better, go through preliminary phases of a relationship to be let down and hurt. We miss the obvious. The obvious, of course, is that we are acting out something within ourselves we have not dealt with. Otherwise, we would not have been attracted to that person in the first place.

A few years ago I met a woman through work whom I found to be interesting, intelligent, funny, eccentric. Over the course of several months, she and I struck up a friendship. We did a lot of things together, everything from concerts to recovery. We even traveled. After awhile I discovered that this woman suffered from multiple personality disorder. There were times when I didn't know which personality I was talking to and, in fact, did not know how to deal with all the personalities involved (I ended up counting five). It was very unsettling.

I felt as though I was constantly learning a new variation on the waltz. I felt I was always being placed in a position of being off balance.

I learned from this experience that I was attracted to this woman's friendship because there was a great deal about her that reminded me of my own father. In my own recovery my father was the more difficult parent for me to deal with. My mother, who was the practicing alcoholic, was easier to deal with. My father, on the other hand, was a different ball game. I never was able to piece together all of the parts that made up his personality, but knowing this woman eventually helped me to better understand. From the objectivity of my sponsor and a couple of other professionals, I was able to equate a lot of this woman's behaviour with the behaviour of my father.

Over the course of time, I came to realize that knowing this woman had been a great gift from the Universe, although I sure didn't see that at the time.

Once we uncover this form of denial, take a look at it, remove the blanket that is covering it, shake it out, dust it off, bring it out of the darkness and into the light, we can see it for what it really is and then say good-bye to it. The bogey man becomes a lot smaller.

We always have those tapes somewhere in our heads. They never totally disappear. We have to monitor ourselves on a daily basis. There is no getting around it.

Those denial tapes may not have been played for a very long time, but given the right set of circumstances they are going to trigger. The difference between now and back then is the trigger won't have as much kick. Our denial system is more thinly veiled and we can grab it, take it out into the sunlight, take a look at it and, hopefully, get rid of it.

Most of us in North America have been brought up with a work ethic. An honest day's work for an honest day's pay. That is a healthy attitude. We owe our employer that because our employer gives us our monthly paycheque. This has created a system of checks and balances that our foundations are built on.

The games that go on within, as mentioned earlier, are ever present. What we owe that employer, of course, is that honest day's work and a good attitude in performing it. That good attitude comes from our own sense of self, and leaves out all of the apple polishing stuff.

If you have a superior who you think is just tickety boo and who you would just do anything for, watch yourself around him/her. By that, I mean, watch your actions. Are you performing your job to the best of your ability? Your attitude is good? You are meeting all the deadlines? Fine. That is all you owe.

Do you ever catch yourself lurking about to see if he needs his/her pencils sharpened, putting yourself in a position to sooth his/her fevered brow, asking too many personal questions about his/her family, trying to place your professional relationship on a more personal level? If you are, the chances are pretty good that you are dealing with something in your own denial system that is triggering your people-pleasing tapes and as a result, going beyond the bounds of your professional work ethic.

This is really easy to fall into. Especially if we have a supervisor who is a really great supervisor. Someone who is an all-round person, cares deeply for other people, has an intelligent approach to his/her job. If we are fortunate enough to work with someone like that and who gives us the added benefit of always saying "please" and "thank you" it is really easy to decide that we are just going to jump through all of those hoops of fire, just to be noticed. You know what? He/she does not expect that from us. And we should not expect that from us, either. He/she is a good supervisor because he/she is coming from a good place within him/herself. If you are a good employee, you are coming from a good place within yourself, as well. If you start to polish the apple, he/she is going to scratch his/her head and wonder what the hell is going on. And somewhere along that line, that professional bonding that has been building between you and him/her begins to erode. Catch it while you can.

Another scenario in the work place is the person who is the schmuck to deal with. If the schmuck is your superior and you need the job, you can find yourself jumping through just as many hoops and polishing just as many apples to keep this schmuck happy. The difference of course is that now you are doing this out of fear and probably giving off signs that, at the same time, your respect level is pretty low. It is only going to be a matter of time before you find yourself at loggerheads. What do you do? You do the best job that you know how and leave his/her baggage to him/her. He/she is the one that has to deal with it, not you, and if there is any spillage over you, mop it up and get it out of there as quickly as possible, and get on with your work. You are lifting that veil of denial.

When that veil of denial begins to lift the fear level will subside. You can take a look around, and begin to examine your options. Maybe there is something else within your working environment that you would like to do. Or, indeed, maybe it is time to look for another job. Or maybe you can just find it within yourself to set your own standards and let the devil take the hindmost.

All of us have people within our working environment that don't meet our personal criteria. That is part and parcel of being there. Do we step aside or do we plow through? That depends on where our denial system is sitting. Once we recognize that our denial system is there and we recognize whether or not we are dealing with it, we make our working lives a great deal easier.

OK. That is about work. That is easy. What about the rest of it?

Well, the toughest part of the denial system, and our awareness level, comes with the people that we love. As our denial systems fall away and our awareness level heightens, it becomes easier to spot where our loved ones are having their own problems.

We need to take a look at the dynamics of the relationship within the family and deal with it accordingly.

I have two grown daughters. For many years I was really good at giving them advice. Advice that neither wanted nor needed. But, boy, was I good at it.

What I learned through recovery was that they didn't want my advice. They wanted my support. They have their own journeys. Their journeys, if I have been a good parent, is to allow them to grow at the level they are most comfortable with.

Sometimes we don't agree. How many mothers and daughters do you know that do agree? More and more I found myself saying "it is up to you". "You have to make the decision that feels right for you."

My daughters vacillate between their own denial systems and their own awareness levels on a regular basis, the same as I do. I don't want to lock horns, or be right. I just want to love them. I want them to love me back, on my terms. My terms are that I am a unique individual doing the best that I can with the tools that I have and I expect to be honoured for that. They may not agree with me, or I them, but I do expect honour, because I honour them. We have a win/win.

We can't reach those special places of honour if each of us is unaware of ourselves and the people around us. With honour, the love continues to build.

I cannot fix either of my daughter's pain, for whatever reason, nor can either of my daughters fix mine. I can, however, support them through their painful periods, as I expect they will support me through my painful periods.

I can honour their judgment calls as I expect they will honour my judgment calls and I can respect mistakes as I, in turn, expect them to respect my mistakes.

We are, after all, only human. Our awareness levels will continue to heighten as the years go by.

What do we do when we find ourselves in denial? We give each other lots of space. I'm not even sure how that evolved. But it has evolved. We honour each other's need for privacy and space. By granting each other that space, eventually the denial begins to break down and the awareness surfaces.

We will always have disagreements about various aspects of our lives. That we respect each other's differences is the ultimate key. By respecting each other's differences, we continue to bond more closely.

As parents, what do we want? Hold on tightly, or let go lightly?

We know from bitter experience, being at both ends of the stick, that if we hold on tightly we are going to lose. If we let go lightly we are going to gain. It always works that way.

I think parenting is the most difficult and the most rewarding job of any relationship. I decided, long ago, that God made us parents to teach us unconditional love and forgiveness. We go through this on a daily basis. We love our kids because of what they are, not in spite of what they are. Very often things we see in our kids that we don't like or disapprove of are exact mirrors of what we see in ourselves and haven't learned how to deal with. That is where the circle simply must be broken! We have absolutely no choice but to break that circle.

If we continue to pass our denial down from generation to generation we will have a lot of problems in our families, and our society, than we already have, if that is possible.

If we honour our children's mistakes, attitudes, thinking, we validate them. By validating them we give them room to grow. The more room they have to grow the more aware they become. The circle takes on a different meaning. The best way to teach that is by practicing it ourselves.

We practice this the same way we practice everything else. One Day at a Time.

If we are stuck in our denial then we go on to the next step, which is Twelve Steps. Break down whatever problem we are experiencing on the basis of the Twelve Steps and work it through. From one end of the circle to the other, until we are back where we started, One Day at a Time, only this time, we are on a much healthier level.

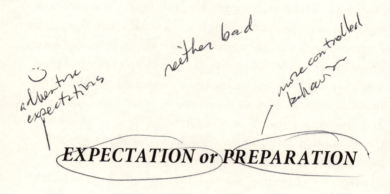

EXPECTATION or PREPARATION

Do you find yourself in a situation, look around and say "I don't know why I feel this way about it." "I knew this was going to happen." "Now that it has happened, I just feel helpless." "I feel so worthless and out of control." "I am so angry, so invalidated, so hurt." And the list goes on.

One of life's paradoxes is that life is much better if we live it one day at a time, but we also have to make plans for tomorrow. This is one of the Fine Lines of Wellness of learning to live with ourselves.

Here is an example. I worked with a woman who was expecting her first child. She had never been around children. Neither had her husband. She did not appear very excited about having this baby. She had been heard to say that she did not like children, or she was nervous around children, or she did not know what to do with them. I personally felt she would make a wonderful mother, and her nervousness and fear were just that. As the pregnancy progressed, she became more aware of the changes in her body, and less aware of why. The last day at work, she started to have "cramps". She came into the office about 8:30 in the morning complaining about them. Her co-workers suggested, quite strongly, that she should at least be calling her doctor if not going to the hospital. She said "no" they were "cramps" and she was going to deal with that accordingly.

We had planned on giving her a surprise shower on her final afternoon and give her a stroller and a few other items. When she walked into the room we all began to clap and cheer. She immediately broke into rears, ran from the room, and came back a few minutes later to tell us that she blamed it all on her hormones and the fact that she was having these "cramps". She was very happy to be accepted by her co-workers, and very touched by the gifts.

We later learned she gave birth to a baby girl the following day.

We also learned that the only thing she had for this baby were gifts that had been given. No diapers. No shirts. No blankets. None of the stuff that babies need when they come home from the hospital. For the first few days her husband was very busy chasing all over town buying things and getting the nursery in working order. Everything worked out OK.

Her husband was very supportive. She received support from her family and friends and she is, of course, a very fine mother.

This story illustrates the point that here is a woman that, for eight months, knew that she was expecting a child and did absolutely nothing to prepare for it. Because she didn't know what to do.

I think a lot of us go through life not knowing what to do. We don't know how to prepare for what it is that we need.

When we grow up in dysfunctional families we learn to live very much for the moment, because that is what we need to do to survive.

If dad comes home drunk and dangerous, we need to know how to get out of his way. If mother kisses us one day and slaps us the next, we need to learn how to tiptoe around her moods. If Uncle Harry comes home late one night and crawls into bed with us, and we are sexually molested, we will react and then shut down.

These are the tools we carry from childhood to adulthood. These reactive tools that have now become weapons.

By the time we are in our thirties, a lot of us learn that these survival tools just don't work anymore. Our reactive and undisciplined behavior is creating a whole lot of problems for us.

In recovery, we learn things like healthy discipline. With healthy discipline we now can learn how to prepare.

If I told you, in a very bitter voice, that my life didn't turn out the way I wanted because I had always wanted to be a concert pianist. I wanted to play on the stages of the world and have people tell me how wonderful I was. This was something I never achieved and it went a long way to ruining my life.

You may look at me and say "gee, that is too bad". "What went wrong?" I would tell you that in fact I had only four years of music.

You may be too polite to say anything but your thoughts would be saying "well, silly woman, what does she expect?" "She only had four years of music." "How can she expect to be a concert pianist?" "That makes no sense."

And, of course, you are right. It does not make sense.

I cannot become a concert pianist if I am not prepared to sit down at a piano on a daily basis, and work the scales, and continue to search out and learn from very dedicated and talented teachers.

I have to prepare myself for that big break. Because, if I don't prepare myself that big break is never going to happen.

If I want to be the best surgeon I can be I have to be prepared to spend a lot of money, go to very good schools, study hard, and spend lots of late nights and early mornings, for about 12 to 15 years and maybe, just maybe, all that hard work and tenacity will give me my big break, and I will become a very good surgeon.

Perhaps my talents aren't in music or surgery. Perhaps I am just looking at pies in the sky.

I must be prepared to look at what my talents are.

When we come from dysfunctional backgrounds that disallow us to search for our talents, we have to spend some time getting in touch with ourselves.

This can be a very difficult process. Because, one of the ways we have learned to survive is to disassociate ourselves with ourselves. Now we have to get in touch. A big job.

How else are you going to learn about your talents?

There is another Universal Truth that says everyone has a talent that contributes to the whole.

If, as children, we were allowed to explore the talents we were given, talents that were meant to be used for our own happiness and contributions as a whole, I would not have had to write this book. And you would not have to read it.

Now, however, our level of self awareness is such that we can look at ourselves and say "I am talented" in certain areas. We can now utilize and exploit those talents. We can prepare ourselves for our big break, and share our talents with ourselves and with the whole. And, you know what?

We do this, ONE DAY AT A TIME.

Statistics say that the lifespan of the average North American is now well into the 70's and 80's. Statistics also say that most people retire at the age of 65. We don't need to be rocket scientists to figure out that this is going to give us ten years or more in which we are not going to be earning the income we are presently earning, and we still want to live at the lifestyle to which we have grown accustomed.

So, what do we do? We prepare for it. We can prepare for this by setting aside money in a monthly retirement account. Perhaps we can buy property we would like to live in. We can get re-training. We can exploit another talent so that we can keep ourselves busy and productive during our retirement years. We can quit smoking so that we will have a better quality of life. We can give up junk food, and go for a daily walk. We can get involved in group and community activities that may be new to us.

Perhaps we still have teenage children. The oldest is now talking of going to university and leaving the city.

The younger child has two or three years before he/she will be doing the same thing. Barring any unforeseen circumstances, within three years, we won't have any more kids around. We will have their bills. But we won't have the kids. That is going to create a vacuum. How are we going to fill it?

We look at our talents and then look around for a place where we can utilize them, and we begin to prepare.

A loved one is terminally ill. The doctors don't know how long the person will be with us. The prognosis is that our loved one will only live for a short period of time but the doctors don't know if it will be a year or three.

We begin to prepare for living our lives after the death of our loved one. One Day at a Time.

To prepare ourselves for living our life, we must ensure that our loved one has a Will. All of his/her affairs are in order. That he/she is physically, mentally and spiritually comfortable, and that we are nurturing ourselves.

We do this One Day at a Time.

We continue to do this while we expand our own support group. When it comes time for our loved one to leave, we are prepared. We have our own grieving system in place so that we can go through our grief steps. It is never easy.

Something can happen out of the blue and we have to deal with it right now. But, as we prepare ourselves for other eventualities, that "accident factor" of other things happening, can take on different meanings. Because we have been preparing ourselves at other levels within our lives, be it going to school or to exploit a talent, we are in better shape to handle these emergencies.

By preparing for the birth of a new child, or retirement, or a loved one's departure, or any other circumstance that we know of, our preparation has allowed us to have more tools in our tool box. As our own growth expands and the "accident factors" happen, we are able to deal with them from positions of strength. Because we are stronger from within.

We cannot prepare for anything alone. We need help. It does not matter what undertaking we have decided on. We need help in achieving our goal.

If we want to be a concert pianist, we need good teachers. If we want to be a fine surgeon, we need good teachers. If we want to write a book, we need people around us who will support our endeavours. If we want to save money for our retirement, we need to talk with financial experts. If we want to exploit a talent, we need experts in that field to show us how to do it.

And, if we are dealing with someone who is terminally ill, we need people around us to help us with the journey.

Of course, we will be doing a lot of work alone, but we need the people out there or in here to keep us on our path.

We continue to do this One Day at a Time, trust in our Higher Power, and let the rest go.

Sounds easier when we do it that way, doesn't it?

It does get easier as we go along. But in the beginning it really takes practice. It is kind of like learning those damn scales on the piano.

Of course, it is impossible to prepare for every eventuality that will happen. We can't do that. It is really important to know that all we can do is the best that we can do and leave the rest behind. This is how we become responders rather than reactors in our world. We strike a balance that we can live with and then do what needs to be done.

Tenacity needs to go along with talent. Don't try and be a concert pianist if you are tone deaf. It won't work. Don't try to become an artist working in oils if you are colour blind. It won't work. Work with what you have.

Maybe you are the best bubble blower in your city.

You know the story about the man who blew these absolutely fantastic bubbles. He is written up in the Guinness World Book of Records and he has also been on Oprah. He started blowing bubbles because they fascinated his children. He ended up able to live a very comfortable life because he could teach other people how to blow these magnificent bubbles.

I think that talent is often related to how people feel about their work. Have you ever noticed that most people, in fact, do not like what they are doing?

Going to work is a means to an end. It pays the rent or mortgage, allows him/her to get drunk on a Friday night and forget about it. Because so many people don't like what they do, they often don't know how to be disciplined in the "right" direction nor do they know how to exploit their own talents.

Imagine what it would be like to get up every day and do exactly what you wanted to do for the rest of that day? To be productive, honest and happy at what you are doing, is truly a state of abundance. The very best way to get there is to find out who we really are, and we do this through working on our recovery.

If we do not do that, we are still playing the same song and doing the same dance of going to work, earning a living, coming home to pay the bills, to get drunk or high on a Friday night, to forget what we do.

There is a big difference between living day to day and living One Day at a Time. Living day to day gets us nowhere. Living One Day at a Time gets us everywhere.

ADDICTIONS or HABITS

We all know what addictions are. Don't we? Of course we do!

Addictions are alcohol, street drugs, prescription drugs, cigarettes, sugar. Addictions that all of us are familiar with. Substance addictions. And now, we can add cell phones and other electronic devices to this list.

Adult Children have at least one of these addictions. And usually more. My big addictions were cigarettes and sugar. I would go through hell trying to quit smoking, and after two or three weeks of feeling like a violin string, I would begin to feel sane again, place myself in a situation where I was primarily surrounded by non smokers and deal with it accordingly. Six months or a year down the line, I would get a notion in my head that I could have that one or two cigarettes with a friend and it wouldn't bother me a bit. I could rationalize this forever. And it did not work. I was a chronic quitter, starter, quitter, where cigarettes were concerned. The day I said to myself "I am an addict – and I can only do this One Day at a Time", that was the day I quit. That was 22 years ago.

I could also get sugar into my system, which would set up the need for more sugar, and I would keep at it until I got on the scales, said "Oh, my God", climb off the scales, take the sugars and fat out of my diet and lose some weight. After about 72 hours I would not have any sugar cravings until I see ice cream. Then it is game over. Ice cream is my drug of choice.

There are different additions that we are only recently beginning to recognize.

We can be addicted to work, bad relationships, sex, chaos, stuff. We can and do get addicted to a great many things.

The experts in the field of addiction tell us that each of us with addictive personalities will replace one addiction with another addiction.

For instance, I did not know I had an eating disorder until I quit smoking.

I know people who have taken up running when they quit smoking. They do not feel right unless they run five or ten kilometers a day. That's a lot of kilometers. A lot of wear and tear on the joints. More than one of these people has suffered permanent damage as a result of trading in their cigarettes for their addiction to running.

I don't think cigarettes are a great thing. They do us an incredible amount of damage, cost a lot of money, smell awful, turn non-smokers off, and generally add to the pollution of our environment.

I have never tried smoking marijuana; because, with my addictive personality, I am very concerned that if I try it, I may become instantly hooked and then I would have to add that to my list of addictions.

A nice thing about choices is that we do have that choice before the addiction sets in. Once the addiction sets in, its a whole lot more difficult to get out of it than it is to make the choice in the first place.

In my mind, compulsions and addictions run parallel to each other. We have talked about this in another chapter, where people become compulsively active in a sport or a project and how they can use it for their betterment or their detriment, depending on the strength of their own wills.

It seems to me that the difference between addictions and habits is a matter of degree.

One of the ways to find out what your addictions are is by sitting down with a piece of paper and, instead of saying, I am addicted to ....., write "I am in the habit of ...." and then fill in the blank. "I am in the habit of lighting a cigarette after I eat." "I am in the habit of grabbing a cup of coffee each time I go by the coffee machine." "I am in the habit of dropping into the neighbourhood pub every Friday night and drinking til closing time."

By making a list of so-called negative habits it doesn't take long to delineate our addictions.

This works for substance addictions as well as emotional addictions. "I am in the habit of choosing the wrong partner." "I am in the habit of getting angry and lashing out in an uncontrolled way." Whatever.

Where do we draw the line?

Substance addictions are easier to spot when we take the denial away from ourselves. Unfortunately, they are a lot easier to spot in other people than they are in us. But if we sit down with that piece of paper and lay our emotions bare, and work from a place of total honesty, some of our denial system will come away and addictions will spring forth on that piece of paper.

Then, what do we do?

We have to get rid of those addictions.

If it is a substance addiction, we join AA or NA and start working the program One Day at a Time. We may even have to enter a treatment centre for awhile.

If it is a cigarette addiction, I have learned through vast experience that the best way to kick that is to set up a time when I knew that my life wold not have too much angst in it, and I could concentrate on breaking the addiction. One Day at a Time.

If it is a sugar addiction, and I can't zip up my jeans, then it can become a matter of vanity and I will start eating properly. If I didn't lick it the first time, I will try and try again. And I do this One Day at a Time. Sometimes we have to break our addictions down to an Hour at a Time. Sometimes I have to break the addiction down to Fifteen Minutes at a Time.

That piece of paper can be all important.

So, what about habits? Well there are good habits and bad habits. This is not a perfect world and we are not perfect people. We can only take a look at our own habits, decide which ones we want to keep, which ones we need to break, and begin dealing with them individually.

Addictions are challenging to break. I think habits can be equally as challenging. Because, whatever we give up from our lives, we have to get something back. Nature hates a vacuum. That's a given. So, if we give up something, we now have a hole that needs to be filled. What do we fill it up with? That depends on the habit.

Several years ago I had a friend who had a habit. His habit was heroin. Imagine calling heroin a habit. I've often wondered how that ever got started. Anyway, through the course of events, he was able to kick his heroin habit and replace it with religion. Boy, did he find religion. He was out to save the world. This went on for several years until one day he discovered that religion wasn't working for him, for whatever reasons, and he switched back to heroin. He died an addict.

I think we need to use some common sense.

For women, one of the most powerful tools we have is a credit card. We learn that a credit card can become a weapon and we have overspent. So, what do we do about it? Well, we get a handle on how to use a credit card. Sometimes we have to take drastic measures with that, cut up the credit card, do without until we get our bills paid, and then discover, by beginning to use a credit card, that we need to use it wisely.

It is not very smart to give up something cold turkey without replacing it with something that is going to be of benefit.

Each of us has a trigger of what we know will benefit us over the long term.

I have learned, through personal experience, that there is no better feeling than using my credit card wisely, paying if off every month, and never being in debt. One of my first rules, now, is to never buy anything unless it is on sale. And the second rule is "do I need it?" This isn't infallible, but for the most part, it works really well.

Going around without a credit card gives me a feeling of impotence and I don't like it. I can't even rent a car if I need to do that. Plastic is now a "necessary" part of our lives. And it is up to me as an adult to learn how to use my credit card in an appropriate way.

So, we have habits that concern money. We can either use the habits wisely, or not. Depending on where we are physically and emotionally.

We have habits on a daily basis. We get up at a certain time. We listen to a certain radio station as we get ready for work. We will climb into the shower at a given time in the morning. We will even buy the same soap to shower with.

Household chores are done on a certain day. We see certain friends in certain ways. We each have certain cleanliness or non-cleanliness habits that we take for granted.

By and large, most of our lives are made up of a long list of habits that we place into operation the moment our feet hit the floor in the morning. And some of those habits even extend into the middle of the night.

Habits are parts of us that other people recognize as who we are, and who we, ourselves, recognize as being our own personalities.

Because habits are part of our personalities and are intrinsically woven through the fibers of our lives, habits can be equally as difficult to break as addictions.

If we need to break some habit we had better find something that is going to fill the void, and quickly, before we fill one bad habit with another bad habit, and continue on in a vicious circle.

Some habits are really endearing. Some are really annoying.

Have you ever worked with someone who whistles between his teeth? God, that can drive a person around the bend in very short order. Here you are, sitting in front of a computer, or at a desk, trying to get paper shuffled all over the place and the person in the next cubicle is habitually whistling away, totally unconcerned that he is bothering or breaking the concentration of the people around him.

What is one of the most common complaints that you hear?

Women talk about men having the habit of leaving the toilet seat up. A lot of women have fallen in the hole in the middle of the night and have had more of a rude awakening than they expected. It can be a real bone of contention.

I don't think there is anybody that doesn't have at least one or two annoying habits. And you notice it more with some people than with others.

Sometimes someone else's habit doesn't have an impact on us. But that same habit will impact someone else.

How do we get ourselves into a place of forming good habits?

I think good habits begin to form when we begin to like ourselves, honour ourselves and feel comfortable within our own skins. Then, we just want to do the best we can for ourselves, so that we can be comfortable with who we are, and who we have become. This, in turn, leads to more productive lives.

Exercise is a good example of this.

When we decide to put ourselves on an exercise program, we need to choose something that we like to do. If we don't want to run the four minute mile, then we don't take up running. If we like to walk in the park, we need to find a friend, or a big dog, and begin to walk in the park. After awhile this becomes a habit. If you get a great deal of satisfaction by going to the gym and working out with weights and sitting in the hot tub later, you might want to make that a habit you can participate in.

It's been my experience that this is an easy habit to break, though. And It's a habit that is always re-forming. I have always had to get myself back in the habit of exercise. It is an ongoing mind set.

If you are in the habit of arriving late for work every day, it is a really good idea to get in the habit of setting your alarm clock 15 minutes earlier, catching an earlier bus or train, or pulling out of the driveway 10 minutes earlier, so you can arrive at work on time. Don't ever kid yourself, that good habits go unnoticed. Bad habits are the first thing to be noticed, of course, because they stand out the most, but good habits follow a close second. When we are out there earning a living it is really important to pull out good habits and stick with them. Good habits such as punctuality, reliability, honesty, discretion, confidentiality, helpfulness, are all noticed in the workplace. They will create an environment for you that will eventually lead to a promotion, more money, more stability, and so on. Bad habits, of course, have the opposite effect.

If we are chronically late, take extended coffee breaks, are never willing to pitch in, gossip about our co-workers, whistle through our teeth, don't bathe every day, look rundown at the heels, that is going to be noticed. We put our jobs in jeopardy. We get passed by for promotion. Our salary will stay stuck and we can't keep up.

These are all choices we have to make.

Do we want the good habits or the bad habits?

Most of us fall between the cracks somewhere along the way. There will be something in our working environment that we don't do to the best of our ability. That can often happen because of work politics. There is no escaping work related politics. They are just there.

Now we can create the habit of not being involved in the politics or putting our noses in where our noses don't belong. We have that choice. If we get involved in the politics of our work place we better be prepared for the flack. If we mind our own business, we may become the unseen worker for awhile, but eventually it will catch up with us and we will be rewarded accordingly.

We get to choose our own habits.

If you are stuck in your workplace and you are not making the kind of advancements you had hoped to make, and all things being equal, and you haven't had any monetary recognition for awhile, ask yourself why. The exception to this, of course, is a bad economy. If we are lucky enough and skilled enough to remain employed during a bad economy, be grateful for that paycheck and be the best employee you can possibly be. Your actions and habits will help your employer pull ahead financially, and everyone wins.

What habits are you bringing to the workplace that are holding you back?

If you are not too sure, sit down in the cold light of a Saturday afternoon and make that list. You will probably surprise yourself at what is staring back at you. You may shake your head and decide to clean up your act, whatever your act happens to be.

If you find yourself involved in office politics, ask yourself "Is this any of my business?" Most of the time it isn't. If you recognize that, back off. We are paid to work, to do the best job we know how and to mind our own business.

It is so important to take a look at our work habits. Because our work habits define our income. Are we the type of employee, for instance, who quits promptly at 5:00 o'clock, regardless of what we are doing? Do we just shut down the computer and catch the 5:10 bus home? Or are we the kind of employee that will stay that extra few minutes to finish whatever we are involved with before the computer is put to bed for the night?

Personally, I preferred to stay and do whatever needed to be done for that five or ten minutes, so I didn't have to face an unfinished project in the morning. I learned that this gave me the reputation of being able to give fast turnaround and placed everyone in a win/win situation. It took me a long time to learn that one.

Be careful of the workaholism trap, here. Five or ten minutes is OK. Not five or ten hours. In my opinion, if anyone is working over fifty hours a week, for any reason, there is a problem. Don't change your habit into an addiction.

A lot is written about burnout these days. If you are over a fifty hour week, check into your local library, or go online, and get some information on burnout. It might help you to break the workaholic habit. If it doesn't, find that all important group, so you can find out why you are setting yourself up that way.

What about our habits at home?

We often come home at night feeling tired, distraught, fed up. How do we deal with that?

Some of us deal with it by putting on old clothes, plopping down in front of the television set and vegging in front of the news. Some of us deal with it by creating the habit of going for a long walk as soon as we get home. Or, if we are fortunate enough to live close to work, walking to and from work to get our exercise.

We all have choices about how we want to create our own habits.

We choose when we are going to brush our teeth, when we are going to get our hair cut, what kind of skin care products we will use, and how often, what time we are going to eat during the course of the day.

Good habits take the pressure off. Bad habits put the pressure on. If we fall into a pattern of good habits on a daily basis, we and everyone around us can only benefit.

If we have bad habits, on a daily basis, we can only suffer, and those around us will be sucked into our vortex.

We have that choice.

Habits, like anything else, have to be watched every once in awhile. If we are in the habit of doing our laundry every Wednesday night and someone says "God, I've got great concert tickets to see Lady Gaga", and we turn them down because we have to go home and do our laundry, we almost certainly have a problem. We can get so entrenched in our habits that we can become rigid. Our lives will become very narrow and we are going to lose a whole lot of experiences.

That's probably a far fetched example. I mean, how many people would turn down the opportunity to see Lady Gaga? But you get my drift.

If a friend phones at the last minute and it's a beautiful day, and the friend says "let's go to the beach", and you find yourself saying "Gosh, I can't because this is the day I have the habit of doing my vacuuming, or washing the car", think again. Go to the beach. The carpets and the car will wait. You may have an extra hour or so to put in the following day – so what? You may never get another chance to go to the beach with that friend again. Don't pass it up.

Habits have to be flexible. Habits need to be looked at on a fairly regular basis and bad habits need to be broken. And, again, it's really important to take those bad habits and break them up and fill yourself up with good habits. When we begin doing this, we fill our lives with all of the good things that we need.

We need good habits because we need structure. Without structure we are totally fragmented. The structure needs to be mobile enough to allow us to move. Without that mobility the structure will become cemented. When that happens we become totally inflexible and the structure can cave in on us. Back to the tent pegs.

It is important that we look at this issue regularly and deal with it according to our emotional needs at the time.

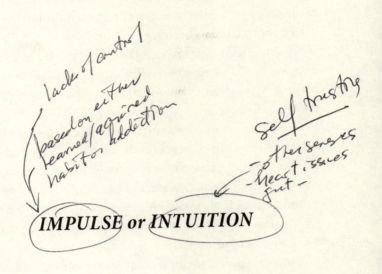

IMPULSE or INTUITION

How do we know the difference between Impulse and Intuition?

We can act on impulse very quickly, within seconds. Within those few seconds we can create a situation for ourselves that we had no idea of creating in the first place. We do the same thing with intuition.

What is the difference?

Impulsiveness goes hand in hand with being reactive. As we have seen in another chapter, every day of our lives we are presented with challenges. Some of these challenges are minor and some are major. No two days are alike.

We build our lives around a set of certain circumstances because uniformity very often gives us all a healthier base to work from. We get up at a certain time, eat breakfast (or don't) at a certain time, go to work via the same route, do our jobs in a certain fashion, have certain hobbies and outlets that we follow on this daily and weekly path. We will watch Monday night football faithfully, go to the gym on Tuesday and Thursday, play Bridge on Saturday and even make love at certain times of the day and certain days of the week.

For those of us overcoming reactive environments this kind of life becomes deadly dull. So we go about creating various sets of circumstances that allow us to act on impulse. Because impulse changes the tedium of our lives, as we see it, and gives us that certain rush we need so we can feel alive.

Almost without exception, impulsive behaviour creates a negative outcome.

Impulsive buying, for instance, can really create a lot of chaos with your bank account and charge cards. There you are, walking through a mall, on your way back to work, and you spot that absolutely perfect jacket that you know you simply cannot live without. So, what do you do? You run in, check the size, slap it on your charge card, hurry back to work with your precious new possession and have a fainting spell when the bill comes in.

If you re-wind this to ten minutes before you passed that store, you realize that jacket you can't live without, wasn't even in your mind until you saw it. If it wasn't in your mind until you saw it, then how come, in one split second, it has become the most important thing in your life?

We do these impulsive things in all sorts of different ways.

How many times have you found yourself in a situation on your job, when things aren't going the way you wanted them to go. There are cutbacks in your organization, there is a wage freeze, there is a co-worker that is just as obnoxious as hell to be around. You walk into the bathroom, throw your hands over your hand, and say "I quit!". At least I hope you walk into the bathroom, throw your hands over your head and say "I quit!". Better to walk into the bathroom and do that than walk into your boss's office saying the same thing. Once you say it to your boss you gotta go through with it.

If you say it to a toilet or a urinal, you can take the words back.

Often compulsive behaviour comes from anger. When someone you care about reacts negatively to a situation that is happening between the two of you, it is really easy to impulsively lash out and say hurtful things that we cannot take back, but will leave deep, bleeding wounds that take a long time to heal.

If we become accustomed to acting on impulse through childhood and adolescent tapes, it is an extremely difficult habit to break.

While I was writing this book I was watching a member of my ow family deal with her impulsive behaviour. She and I have the most incredible conversations. Within five minutes she can, in her mind, move to another city, change careers three times, get another boyfriend and decided to dye her hair. She knows that she is very impulsive. She also knows that her impulsiveness has led her down some very difficult paths. Some of these paths have led her to places that she had no intention of going. Because she has dealt with this impulsive behaviour most of her life, she has become aware that she needs to monitor it very carefully and can only do that on a daily basis. She now sets some goals for herself and works towards them. I think that she will always be somewhat impulsive. In fact, her impulsive behaviour often makes her a very interesting person. I never know what to expect. However, her impulsiveness has, more often than not, kept her from reaching goals that she has set for herself.

One day she said "I feel like I am in jail". That remark came about because of an impulsive act that will cause her a good deal of inconvenience for the next two or three years.

I really relate to what she went through, because I've been there, in spades.

There has been more than one occasion in my life where I wished I had gone into the bathroom, thrown up my hands and said "I quit" to the toilet, instead of going into the boss's office and doing the same thing. There has been more than one instance in my life when I have lashed out at someone I love without thinking of the consequences, and leaving very deep scars. I really relate to what she's going through.

The upside of this impulsive behaviour is a pattern that both she and I recognized. I do what I can for my impulsive behavior patterns, she does what she can do for hers, and up to this writing, we talk to each other. We talk about the progress or lack of progress with this particular problem. Because we share this common bond, neither of us judges the other. That non-judging has been, for both of us I think, a great tool in helping each of us overcome our mutual pattern.

The overt stuff with impulsive behavior is fairly easy to deal with. That spiffy jacket that you can't live without can stay in the store for a day or two until you take a look at your wardrobe, your bank account, and the balance owing on your credit cards. After that, decide if you really need that jacket. Personally, most times I find that it isn't worth the long term sacrifice and the jacket stays in the store.

The angry remarks can be more difficult. Of course, the problem has to be addressed. The air has to be cleared and the relationship has to be healed. But sometimes, in the heat of anger, the words are said and cannot be recovered. The damage is done.

So, what about intuition? What is the difference?

The best definition I ever heard for intuition was the definition of Arnold Patent's. He said that the definition of intuition is God talking to us between our thoughts. That's an interesting concept, isn't it?

The more that we get in touch with who we are, the more we honour our own selfhood, the more finely tuned our senses become, the more we begin to understand how our intuition works.

Have you ever had the experience of having someone pop into your mind, someone you haven't thought about for months or even years, and within a matter of hours or days, you will run into that person on the street?

Have you ever had the experience, while driving your car, of looking over to your left, well before you get to the intersection, only to see that guy shoot a stop sign? If you hadn't looked you would have been schmucked. That's intuition.

Have you ever had a real inescapable urge to call someone in your family whom you haven't spoken with for a long time, pick up the phone, and find that they are in distress? That's intuition.

Each of us, without exception, has that tiny inner voice, deep within our souls, that tells us exactly what we need to know.

Most of us are so busy covering up that tiny voice with layers of denial and ego that we miss our intuitive natures a good deal of the time. By missing out on our intuitive natures, we are short changing ourselves to such a degree that it's almost impossible to fathom.

I truly believe that we cannot lead rich, rewarding lives until we acknowledge our intuition. Our intuition comes from a Higher Power who knows infinitely more than we do. If we trust that Higher Power there is no way that we can go wrong.

The trick is in the definition.

If we are acting on impulse and blame it on intuition, we are short changing ourselves.

Intuition has to come from within. Impulse comes from without. There are no exceptions.

If we feel very strongly about something, and we acknowledge and honour that strength, there is only one thing we can do. And that is to act on that strength, go forward with it, and succeed.

When we act on impulse we react from without, and go backward, and fail.

This is a real cosmic joke, I think, and we often have trouble defining the difference.

A neat thing that happens with intuition is that we develop a keen sense of healthy spontaneity. Spontaneity brightens up our lives, makes us more interesting individuals and creates a more sparkling atmosphere for ourselves and for those around us. Spontaneity can manifest itself in a good sense of humour, off the cuff remarks, quick shows of affection, a helping hand when someone slips, all sorts of things that we do in the course of a day, a week, a month, a lifetime.

When we marry our spontaneity and our intuition we are in pretty good shape.

How do we get into our intuition? We've been so busy beating off the bogey man (ourselves) all these years. Now we are at the point in our lives where we recognize who the bogey man is (ourselves) and it is time to learn the skill.

How do we do that?

Most people I know find the answer to their intuition through meditation.

"Hey, wait a minute" you're saying. "If I wanted to read a book on metaphysics, religion, philosophy, I would have bought a book on any one of those things". Most of us have some pretty hard and fast preconceived ideas about what meditation is. It's the guy sitting at the top of the mountain, cross legged in a loin cloth, saying he's got the answer to life, isn't it?

As far as I know, that only happens in people's imagination. If any of you out there know differently I'd sure like to hear about it.

Meditation means a whole lot of different things. There are the obvious ways of doing it. Take a look in your adult education courses or through a calendar of events in your neighbourhood and you will probably find a meditation course that someone is teaching.

There are all sorts of other ways to meditate. Did you know that you can meditate by going for a long walk along a beach or through the forest? Did you know that you can meditate by putting on soft music, reclining in your favourite chair with your eyes closed, and just allow the sounds to wash over you? Did you know that you can meditate by watching a sunset or a sunrise, depending on the direction you face, and what your body clock is used to? Did you know that you can meditate while you are doing your morning run? Did you know that you can meditate while you are pumping iron at the gym?

All of these, and many, many other activities will slow your frontal brain (otherwise known as your Committee of Assholes), allow your back brain to kick in, and give you answers that you weren't even aware that you possessed. Try it.

Pick an activity that you do on a fairly regular basis. Walking the beach, pumping iron, golfing, playing tennis, doing yoga, listening to music.

Choose a small problem that has been niggling at you and that your Committee has left wandering in the frontal part of your brain – a problem that you have not been able to come to terms with. Now, take that problem and tuck it away.

You can do this physically if you need to. But it is best to do this physically with no one else around. Because, if someone else is seeing you do this they will think you are off your rocker. If you think it is necessary, put your hands up to your forehead. Ask the problem to come out into your hands. Look at the problem that is now in your hands. Take your hands around to the back of your head, and imagine the problem settling there. Now go on to the meditative active that you have chosen.

If that problem should begin to surface while you are performing that activity, just gently remove it. Say to it "no, I don't want to deal with you now, I'll deal with you later", and continue on with the activity. At the end of the activity you will begin to get insight into what you need to do to handle the problem. You may have to repeat the activity. If you do, that's fine. Sometimes we get in the way of ourselves and need to listen for a while longer.

If you decide to go through this exercise before a game of tennis and you don't have the answer to the problem at the end of the set, just continue to put the problem back there, and if you are playing tennis for three days this week, the answer will come to you sometime during the next three days. If not, just repeat the process. Because you are the only one holding up the correct answer. So, while repeating the process, get out of your own way.

Now, there is a trick to this. You take the problem from the front of your head (that Committee of Assholes), place it in the back of your head and quit concentrating on the problem. You want to concentrate on the solution. That is where the answer is found. So you say to yourself "I need a solution to this particular challenge". Concentrate on the word "solution".

100 % guaranteed that you will get the answer. It may not be the answer that you thought. Very often it isn't. But it will be the answer you need. And it may not even be all of the answer, it may only be part of it. That's OK. You are only meant to work on that part of the answer that was given to you.

Take the next part of the problem, do exactly the same thing, turn it to the back of your head, concentrate on the solution, and work on stage two.

Pretty soon the problem won't be there anymore. More often that not, the problem disappears without a whole lot of effort from us. You know why? We got out of the way. And that is where our intuition is. If we get ourselves out of the way, put our egos aside and say "I can't do this, I need help from my Higher Power", we ask for that help, that help is going to come to us. It is a Universal Truth that cannot be ignored, and it works every time.

Doesn't that sound a whole lot better than impulse?

Lots of people have been doing this for a long time without even knowing that they are doing it. We've all heard stories of people who bought stock at the right time, found their dream house by just turning a certain corner, saw the perfect car for themselves on a lot across the street, "accidentally" bumped into their mate, "stumbled" into exactly the right job. The list is never-ending.

It takes a lot of concentration, and non-concentration at the same time. You have to concentrate on putting it away for awhile before you can take it out and look at it. And that's the fine line.

The more we allow our intuition to kick in, the easier our lives are. If we are used to chaos, we will go back to impulse just to mess things up for a little while, because we are comfortable in that role. But somewhere along the line, we discover that we may be used to it, but we don't like it, and we go back to developing our intuition.

Kind of like learning how to play the piano, isn't it? Practice makes perfect.

After awhile it becomes effortless effort, and it will never let you down.

INTEREST or CURIOSITY

Healthy interest is a wonderful thing. It gets us out of ourselves, allows us to reach out and experience events around us, growth patterns within us, and generally acts as a magnificent tool to enrich our lives.

Without interest we would be back in the stone age, fall into complacency and generally lead humdrum existences.

Before we get into the joys of being interested, let's explore the downside of curiosity.

Curiosity can become a weapon we can all do without. And it is an easy trap to fall into.

This type of curiosity comes about when people are so concerned, at a deep level, with keeping themselves shut down that it becomes all important to them to know as many intimate details they can about other people's lives.

They take the information they have gleaned, twist it out of proportion and gossip ensues.

Gossip is vicious and denigrating. It is vicious because it is filled with only half truths, is extremely dangerous, and denigrating, not only to the person to whom the gossip is aimed, but also to the person who is speaking the gossip.

There is no concern in gossip. None at all. If we were concerned for another person we wouldn't gossip about them.

Once we figure out the difference between interest and curiosity it is fairly easy to delineate between the two.

A curious person will put on an act of being your best friend, prod you with questions, get the answers that she thinks she hears, then take that information and try to use it as a control mechanism. If that control mechanism doesn't work the person will resort to gossip to continue on in the controlling scenario, usually by telling tales out of school.

Either way, the curious busy body still feels like she is in control. You see, no one is curious for our own benefit. She is only curious for her own benefit. The two are not mutually compatible.

Curious people do not think that anyone has the right to privacy.

Everyone has a right to privacy. There are no exceptions. Curious people, however, don't recognize that right. They would rather take as much of your time and energy as possible to figure out exactly what makes you tick. They're not interested in what makes you tick on the inside, but are more interested in the external persona for the sole enjoyment of pointing fingers and laying blame.

Do any of us want this in our lives? I don't think so. Do any of us have this in our lives? Every one of us.

We all suffer from the negative effects of curiosity. Not only do we suffer from it with other people, but we fall into the trap ourselves.

For instance, tabloid newspapers are the biggest sellers on the North American and English markets. What are tabloid newspapers selling? A bunch of nosy details of famous (and infamous) people's lives that we have no business knowing in the first place. Are we any better off for knowing this information? I don't think so.

I lot of people get hurt by the misrepresentations in tabloid newspapers. It is easy to fall into the trap of a tabloid newspaper if our own lives have become so quietly desperate that we can't figure out any way of overcoming it. It has now become fairly easy to dish the dirt about somebody else.

It all boils down to that old saw – if we are not part of the solution, we are part of the problem.

Most of us have a busy body in our neighbourhood. If we are lucky, we only have one or two. These people make it a point of knowing as many intimate details as they can garner, real or perceived, about their neighbours so they will have interesting stories to talk about to anybody who appears interested in listening to them.

My own straw poll of this type of behaviour suggests that, more often than not, the people involved in being curious, usually have giant sized control problems that walk hand in glove with their curiosity. As I say, this is my own straw poll and I can't give you any valid statistics from any study that will say I am right or out to lunch.

If any of you are questioning the validity of this statement and wondering if there is some truth to it, take a look at the curious neighbours in your area, or within your family, and then ask yourself if these people also try and control their environment as well as the environments of the people around them. You will probably come up with the same conclusion.

I think that, as professionals begin working more and more within the field of co-dependency and denial, this will be an area that will be looked at in a more serious light. Because it is devastating.

When we are walking around in our own denial systems, and feeling very needy, and not knowing where our boundaries are, it's extremely easy to fall into the trap of the curious friend, curious neighbour, curious relative.

We need someone to talk to. We crave someone to talk to. We are desperately seeking validation that we haven't found in other areas of our lives. When someone says "tell me all about it" and we are so wrapped up in our own pain that we miss the signals, it is really easy to sit there and blurt out intimate details of our thoughts and behaviour patterns to someone who does not have our best interests at heart. I've done it. And I'll bet you've done it as well.

After awhile someone will drop a remark that tells us that this person wasn't coming at us with honourable intentions and we are left with an even deeper scar than when we first trusted them with our most intimate secrets in the first place.

Nosiness is probably where 90% of the mother-in-law jokes come from. If mothers-in-law minded their own business and quit trying to get involved with their offsprings' lives, there would be no jokes to tell.

Fine Lines of Wellness, One Step Beyond Recovery

I remember, as a young girl, a favourite line from my grandmother. "What would the neighbours think?" This left an incredible impression on my psyche.

"What will the neighbours think?" became second nature to the way I reacted, not only within my family, but within the wider sphere of my own community. There was a point in my upbringing when I was so concerned about what the neighbours thought that I tiptoed around my own needs, fell into people-pleasing in a big way, and did everything I could to make sure they had nothing to talk about. From that stance, I went to the opposite side of the coin, said "to hell with what the neighbours think" and proceeded to get myself into more trouble than I knew what to do with. There never seemed to be any happy medium.

My grandmother was not as fault for this. That is the way she had been raised.

I finally realized how ludicrous this statement was over the simple act of washing clothes. I was working, had a husband and a two year old daughter. The only day that I could do my laundry was on a Sunday. My grandmother was visiting us for a week. Sunday morning I announced that I was going to have to do the laundry before we carried on with our plans. The very first thing my grandmother said was "what will the neighbours think?" And she didn't even live there!! That's when it struck me as ludicrous. This was back in the days when I hung my laundry on an outside line so, of course, my neighbours were going to see that I was doing my laundry on a Sunday. Now, of course, lots of people do their laundry on a Sunday because most homes and apartments are furnished with washers and dryers, so our neighbours don't know. And if they did, do we care? Do they care?

Curious people are leading very unfulfilled lives. That is why they are curious.

If we have a handle on that it is a lot easier to keep ourselves from falling into the trap of listening to idle gossip that can sometimes be vicious, and is often twisted. It also keeps us from falling into the trap of being curious ourselves.

When we find ourselves in a position of asking too many questions of an individual, we need to ask ourselves why we are doing it. Are we doing it out of genuine concern, or just simply because we are curious?

Whatever he is dealing with is his problem. If he chooses to share it with us is one thing. If he doesn't, then it is none of our business. It's as simple as that.

I think that concern falls under the umbrella of healthy curiosity.

Pick any Alcoholics Anonymous, Over Eaters Anonymous, or any anonymous meeting anywhere in North America and you will hear stories that can often let your blood run cold. You may hear these stories, you may have a few of your own, but the magic button is the word "anonymous". No one knows who you are unless you choose to break your anonymity. You don't know the other people there, either. The other amazing thing we discover about anonymous groups is that once the meeting is over, people do not talk about any stories they heard. It is a code that should never be broken. The word "anonymous" is sacred. The word "anonymous" simply must be upheld to enable each person within the confines of that group to get on with the business of healing. There can be absolutely no exceptions to this. None of us can get to our own bottom lines unless we feel we are in a safe environment with which to do so. If we do not have our anonymity, we will not feel safe and our bottom line will remain elusive to us.

Is that what we want? I don't think so. Each of us wants more for ourselves and I think, in the final analysis, each of us wants more for our friends and loved ones as well.

Healthy interest, on the other hand, is a whole different ball game. Without healthy interest, everything from the invention of nuclear power to the invention of post it notes would be non-existent. This type of interest has enabled medical science to come out of the dark ages, create new forms of treatment, save millions of lives. This type of interest will ultimately go a long way to saving our planet. When we are interested, we want to learn. When we learn, we discover. When we discover, we also invent. When we invent tools for the betterment of ourselves and those around us, everyone benefits.

Interest is meant to be a noble attribute that is instilled in each of us. It will lead us to our creativity and that will lead us to our own fulfillment.

We need healthy interest to lead healthy lives.

BUILDING A RELATIONSHIP
or TAKING A HOSTAGE

Anyone who is an Adult Child knows how very difficult it is to maintain an ongoing, intimate relationship; a relationship that is healthy, caring and productive.

We also have a tendency to define our relationships within the context of men and women and the relationships that we have with members of the opposite sex, while ignoring the relationships that we build, maintain or destroy within our own family units, with friends and co-workers, and most of all, with ourselves.

When I was going through the most intense period of my Twelve Step Program we had a meeting on a New Years Eve. Holidays, particularly the Christmas holidays, are real tough for all of us. All of us need to look for support to not only get us through but to help us create a happy and healthy environment.

Back to this particular New Years Eve. Each person around the table wanted to verbalize his or her resolutions for the coming year. One of the women said "the most important relationship I can have is the relationship I build with myself". "I know that without this relationship being healthy and whole, I cannot possibly ask for a relationship with anyone else to be healthy and whole." "One does not go without the other."

These words were said to a group of us many years ago and I have never forgotten them. We are all so good at looking outside of ourselves to find the answers, when we need to look deep within us. How can be possibly have a healthy relationship with anyone if we are still dealing with our own baggage? If we are still coming from this premise, we are taking hostages, not building relationships. If we are still using some sort of denial system, if we are still playing the needy victim, the persecutor, the people pleaser, whatever role we are adopting and playing on an ongoing basis and in a negative way, constantly looking around to see how we are satisfying other people's needs, then we are not meeting our own. If we are not meeting our own needs, it is impossible to satisfy anyone else's. It doesn't work that way.

This is an extremely difficult pattern to break. For some of us it will take most of our lives. For others, if they are blessed enough to start early in their lives and get a handle on this, and learn how to love themselves they will enjoy better relationships.

How do we define a good relationship?

A good relationship must be built on trust. Do we trust the other person? We need to define the parameters of trust with the other person. None of us is ever 100% trustworthy. How does the other person fall within our own limits of trust? For instance, if monogamy is right up there on your list, best not to get involved with someone who gets a kick out of sexual experimentation. Besides having different values, it just ain't safe.

Do we like to be with the other person? Honestly and truly like to be with that person? Does being with that person allow us to feel more like ourselves?

This is tricky. If you are with someone and you can't feel like yourself, stop and take a look. Is it you, or is it them? If it's you, pull up your socks. If it's them, get them the hell out of your life.

It is absolutely necessary that each of us be given the honour to be who we are. There are no exceptions to this.

We look for the usual things from our friends and prospective mates like sharing the same music, books, activities, habits. I think it is really important that we take this and go into deeper levels. We need to search deeper levels with people who come into our lives, so we can create a compatible environment where we can truly be ourselves. There has never been a relationship that didn't have a lot of compromises attached to it. These relationships vary from the relationships we have with our parents, to the relationships he have with our children, and the relationships we have with our siblings. Each of these relationships requires a degree of compromise in order to maintain it at a level that is healthy for us and for the other person.

And it takes two. If the other person is not willing to compromise within the confines of the relationship sometimes we have to decide whether or not we want to have that person in our physical space. If the dysfunction and the denial is so great that having the other person within our physical space creates any type of physical or emotional harm, then perhaps it is better to do our forgiveness work and get on with our own lives without these people being physically present.

If, however, we want to continue to build a relationship in our family unit with someone whom we love at a very deep level, we need to take a look at the areas we are willing to compromise.

My younger daughter taught me a lot about compromise. Due to circumstances, she and I had not lived under the same roof for ten years while she was growing up. When she was in her early twenties, Tracey came to live with me and we had, for the first time in our lives, begun to form a bonding relationship. We had a lot of fun. And it was really important for each of us to go through this process so we could bond and feel comfortable with each other. My hope was that we would become better people for it.

To allow this process to develop we have both had to learn to compromise. For instance, her household habits are a lot different from mine. I'm a fuss fart. She is casual. I have this thing about order around me. She is more relaxed. We did not argue about it. My living quarters may not have had the corners cleaned as often as I would like, my schedule was upset now and then, but she and I would never walk that way again. Those corners were there for me to clean when this precious time passed. When I think about it in this context, it becomes really impractical, and a bit ludicrous, to look at our relationship from the context of the odd dusty corner. Priority examination proves to be a lot less difficult.

Of course, we are going to have people in our lives whose ideas and attitudes do not fit with ours.

If we didn't have people in our lives like that we would cease to grow.

We need to take a look at where we are willing to compromise in our attitudes and ideas. If our attitudes and ideas are diametrically opposed and we are setting out to change the other person's attitudes, we need to look at the reason we are doing this. Are we trying to change it out of control? Could be. Are we trying to change it out of fear? Probably. Why are we trying to change it? Is it an idea or an attitude that we know, deep within ourselves is very wrong, or is it an idea or an attitude that we just happen to disagree with?

IF someone believes in something that is not our belief, and their belief is not damaging our belief or anyone's else's, why would we want to change it? If someone's belief system does not put us into an uncomfortable situation, why would we want to change it? That's all part of honouring a relationship.

The more comfortable we become with ourselves the more comfortable we become with others' points of view, and are willing to allow those around us to grow at a rate they can handle. The only thing we need to demand from them, is that they give us the same honour. We too need to grow at a rate we can handle. The scale absolutely must be balanced. This goes with our folks, with our brothers and sisters, with our cousins, with our kids, with our lovers. Straight across the board. It has to go that way.

So, you have been reading this all this time, and you are saying to yourself "but, she's not talking about that relationship we all want with that significant other".

You know what? As I write this I really, truly wish that I could tell you that after years of soul searching and getting to know who I am and what I stand for, I have finally met the perfect man for me, and that the two of us have gone off into the sunset holding hands, and are living happily ever after. I really wish I could tell you that. But I can't.

There is no one in my life. Will there ever be? I hope so. Am I desperately seeking it? No. Did I desperately search for it? Yup. Did it work? No. I have learned that I won't find this until I know who I am, where I am coming from, and get some sort of handle of where I want to go. I need to be comfortable with myself, with my aloneness, activities, family and friends. I need to have that comfort that comes from within. Finally, after many years of self discovery, I am getting there.

That's really the bottom line, isn't it? Good companionship. And we are not talking about companionship, we are taking about COMPANIONSHIP. The companionship that a lot of people seek is companionship that is made up of compromising attitudes. Don't allow yourself to fall into that trap. Please.

Take a look at what you stand for, who you are, where your abilities lie, even where your deficits are and what you are doing about them. If necessary, write everything down on a piece of paper, and don't be hard on yourself. Give yourself credit for all sorts of things. If you are having trouble with this, ask a trusted friend or a sponsor to help you. It's a good idea for each of us to write a list of our personal and physical attributes, and even some attributes that we don't consider as attributes, but other people do.

It is important to write about areas of our lives that we absolutely refuse to compromise with. For instance, if you are a member of a certain church or organization, and it is really important for you to stay a member of that church or organization, put that on your list. Don't deter from that. If you meet someone who interests you, and he/she reveals that he/she thinks your particular church or organization is for the birds, the greatest gift you can give yourself is a backward glance as you leave that person at the nearest street corner. You are not going to change his/her ideas or attitudes. You feel very strongly about this. Why set yourself up?

If there is derision from the other person about your religious and/or ethical beliefs, you are not going to change that. If he/she is deriding you for your religious and/or ethical beliefs, he/she is not going to change and neither are you. Neither one of you will budge. Each of you will continue to dig in your heels, stick out your chins, and continue to lay down the blows. Is that what you want? Probably not. But we all fall into this one.

We meet someone who turns our chemistry buttons, says all the right things, makes all the right moves, and we fail to look a little bit deeper to see if there is something else in there that we truly need to know before we pursue this relationship.

I used to know a woman who married a closet drunk. This was her second marriage. She had absolutely no idea this guy was a closet drunk. She never saw him sober.

Her marriage to this man didn't last very long. And he subsequently died of cirrhosis of the liver. In the meantime, it was a blended family and it left some very deep and hurtful scars. She didn't see it, or didn't want to see it. A lot of people got hurt. There was nothing that could have been done after the fact, but there sure were a lot of things that could have been done before the fact, if the denial hadn't been so firmly entrenched.

I think this is the scariest part of getting into a healthy relationship. We have to take a look and see how far we have broken down our own walls of denial. Because, if we haven't broken them down to a healthy level, we are about to get ourselves into a mess. And none of us wants that. None of us deserves it, either.

Relationships are hard work. We are willing to take a risk and get into a relationship with someone who has the same value system as ourselves, and we still know that we have a lot of work before us.

We are coming from a healthier place if we allow ourselves the privilege of knowing exactly what it is we need to work on and leave the rest behind.

For instance, you may be involved with someone who is perfect for you on an emotional and caring level. That person may also be nocturnal and you, on the other hand, like to be up with the birds. To reach a compromise with something as basic as our twenty-four hour internal clocks can be work. If you like to sing in the shower in the morning, and he/she grunts over his/her first cup of coffee, each of you needs to recognize where the other is coming from, keep your sense of humour, and your distance, get on with the business at hand, until your respective moods level out.

If you meet someone who is at the same place spiritually and emotionally, and you are willing to try and build a relationship, and you discover that the other person has a whole different set of eating habits. You are thinking of becoming a vegetarian, and his/her favourite dinner is a large porterhouse steak, medium rare, baked potato with sour cream, and buttermilk biscuits. Obviously each of you is going to have to make some compromises on a daily basis. That takes work. Are you going to cook two meals a day? Are each of you willing to compromise on your eating habits so that one meal can cover both plates simultaneously? Are you going to try to change him/her? Watch out. His/her eating habits are the way they are for reasons known only to him/her, and it is really none of your business. If he/she needs to redefine his/her eating habits, he/she will do that. If you are trying to change him/her, you had better examine your motives, because 99% of the time you are going to come up with a control issue. And he/she is digging in his/her heels and letting you know on a subliminal level, or not so subliminal level, that you can take your control issues and stuff them. He/she will deal with her eating habits the way he/she wants to. Examine your motives.

All relationships, be it parent or partner, must come from a good place. There is nothing more pleasurable than saying to another human being, "gosh, I'm glad to see you", and really mean it.

If we can do that and build our lives around the relationship we have developed with that person, and still be glad that we have that person as a companion, we have got it made.

One of the hardest lessons I learned about relationships is to never take anyone for granted. A good relationship needs to be worked on every time we are with that person. And again, there are no exceptions to that. The work, of course, is done in degrees. Sometimes the work we have to do on any given day is so small that we fail to see it, but it has to be done.

A relationship is like a garden. If you have a little plot of land out your front door and you want to see some flowers growing there, it's a good idea to get some fertilizer, the right kind of plants and seeds that normally thrive in your area. We know when to tend it, when to weed it, when to leave it alone. We know when to nurture it and when to back off. We know how much sun and shade it needs. We know that if the frost is too thick, it will kill the garden. Relationships are the same way.

Relationships need to be nurtured just like that garden. If we are not nurturing our relationship, we are not nurturing ourselves. If we are allowing the frost to form on the pumpkin, we need to take another look so that we can thaw out this area, before it's too late, and get on with the business of building it.

A healthy garden needs room to grow. A good relationship needs room to grow. A healthy garden needs to be nurtured. A good relationship needs to be nurtured. A healthy garden needs to tended. A good relationship needs to be tended.

Line up your relationships like they were part of your garden. Attend to each one, according to the needs of each season, the lay of the land, and watch your garden grow.

You will receive an abundant harvest..

SENSUALITY or SEXUALITY

Our society places so much emphasis on sex and how people are relating to sex, that we have created a very dangerous imbalance.

Sex is everywhere.

Sex has left the privacy of individuals and gone into the public square. Sex sells. Sex sells newspapers, magazines, books, movies, television shows. Sex is one of the greatest weapons used by Madison Avenue in any advertisement campaign. It's used either blatantly or subliminally, and it's used for everything from liquor consumption to selling children's clothing.

I think sex has become such a popular topic of conversation, such a selling feature, such a blatant way of life, because people have shut down.

When we don't deal with the issues that are within us, and we decide, for whatever reasons, that we are going to continue to live within our denial systems, we have to find an outlet. Very often that outlet is sex.

This is not sex that is committed sex, but sex that is casual. How many people do you know who have not participated in at least one, one night stand? How many people do you know who can tell you on the morning after that it was a fully and truly satisfying experience? That the one night stand made them feel complete? That they were able to carry on feeling nourished? How many people do you know who can say that?

I have never met anyone who can lay claim to that, and that includes myself.

I think the reason our society is so preoccupied with sex is because we have built walls around our sensuality.

Sensuality and sex, on the surface, have very little in common.

Before we get into the exploration of both of these issues, and bring them together, let's take a look at them on an individual basis.

What is sensuality?

Sensuality is dealing with all of our five senses. To deal with them all together, we have to feel. The more we feel, the more sensuous we become. There are all sorts of ways that you can check out your sensuality level. You can do this within the privacy of your own room, and if you feel comfortable, with one or two trusted friends.

These five senses are touch, taste, smell, hearing, sight.

Let's start with the sense of touch. As you look around your living room, how many different kinds of fabrics and surfaces can you see? Take your trusty pen and piece of paper, and begin to make some notes. Note the fabric on your couch, the fabric that is on the toss cushions, the finish on your television set, materials that have been used for floor coverings, various types of woods, any living plants that may be enhancing your living area, any silk plants that you may have sitting around, any pieces of pottery, glass, ceramics.

Make a list of as many different types of fabrics and surfaces as you can within your living area. Now, go over to each item that is on your list. Close your eyes and spend the next minute or two exploring that item with your fingers. Allow your fingers to caress each item on your list. Notice how each item feels against your fingers. Notice where there are curves in the item, the thickness of fabrics, the lushness of carpets, the smoothness of hardware.

Concentrate fully on the item you are presently touching, all the while keeping your eyes closed. As you caress each item in your living room, you will "see" it far differently than you see it with your eyes open.

After each item has been touched, jot down on your piece of paper any type of sensation that the nerve ends in your fingers read back to you.

Here's an example.

I have a shellack vase that came from Korea. The inlay on one side of the vase is some art work depicting two birds sitting in an orange tree. The birds and the tree are made of mother of pearl. When I close my eyes and go over the vase with my fingers I have various sensations. I notice the curve of the vase differently than I do when my eyes are open. The curves of the vase stand out under my fingers in sharper contract than they do to my visual eye. The inlaid mother of pearl has a light rise from the shellac vase itself and, in places, I can feel where the artist made a deeper groove to place a petal when he or she did to place a wing. By going through this exercise with my vase I become more familiar with it than I ever did on a seeing level. I do not get that same kind of feeling contact with my vase just by dusting it. I need to close my eyes and physically "see" it.

If I choose to move to the next item in my living room, keeping my eyes closed, my hand falls on two different cushions on my couch. One is made of a woven fabric that is somewhat rough, but even to the touch, another feels smooth, almost like silk.

Take this several steps further. Do as many objects as you can, all the while totally concentrating on each of them on an individual basis, and then placing your findings on your sheet of paper.

I guarantee that you will have a whole different understanding of the textures within your living area.

If you have a partner, a sibling or a child that you feel comfortable doing this with, sit in front of that person, close your eyes and explore that person's face with your fingers. That face will take on a whole new dimension for you.

How do you feel when you are in a warm bath with lots of bubbles? Have you thought about lighting a couple of candles in your bathroom? Putting on soft music or a meditation? And just allowing the warm water to take over your life?

What types of fabrics feel really good against your skin? How do you feel when you are wearing cotton? How do you feel when you are wearing wool? How do you feel when you are wearing silk? How would you feel if you were wearing burlap?

Check out your feelings next time you are wearing fabrics and see how your body responds to them.

Next, move on to your sense of taste. All of us have heard the story of what happens to a singer when he looks out at the audience and someone in the first row is sucking on a lemon. His mouth will automatically pucker and go dry, and he will not be able to utter a note.

If you're feeling really brave, and you kind of like lemons, it's not a bad idea to slice off a bit of lemon, close your eyes, and suck the juice out of that piece of lemon. Feel what happens to your mouth. Similarly, you can try this with various foods you have in the kitchen.

How does an apple taste if you don't look at it first? Do you like your apples at room temperature or from the fridge?

Have you ever noticed (and I'm sure you have) the different consistencies between a spinach salad and cooked spinach? A spinach salad, to me, tastes wonderful. Cooked spinach, to me, is like eating slimy seaweed.

The same can be said for eggs. Would you rather have a cooked egg or a raw egg?

How do all of these textures affect your taste buds and how do these textures feel within the confines of your mouth?

Try and differentiate as many textures as you can within the necessary food groups.

That, of course, includes drinking fluids. Do you find a cup of tea or coffee more satisfying than, perhaps, a cup of hot water? Why do you suppose that is?

Try and define your taste buds as much as you can. Do your taste buds sing on contact with various foods, or does your mouth just feel mellow because of how certain soft foods feel on your tongue?

If you are eating hot, cooked food, can you tell how your sense of smell ties in with your sense of taste?

Our sense of smell. How often do we use it during the course of a day? I have discovered that everyone I know has a distinctive body and personality odour. That odour can range from a signature perfume on women, ones that I can associate with particular people, to after-shave on men, to the odour of unwashed bodies and too much sweat. And that changes as well.

Have you ever noticed that people's homes smell differently? My home has a different scent than your home, and your home will have a different scent than anyone else's you know. Each one is distinctive in its own character. It all changes, depending on how many people are living under your roof at one time. Try and pick up as many smells as you can. If your sense of smell is something that you feel you haven't fully developed and would like to explore it further, the old blind fold test is the way to go.

Choose items within your home that give off some sort of odour. Choose items from perfume and soap to cleaning products to bedsheets and linens, to smells within your own closet, to the smell of onions simmering on top of the stove.

Take each one separately, close your eyes and notice the smells. If you have a partner that you are sleeping with on a nightly basis, notice how her sense of smell, her body chemistry changes from the night before to the morning after. God knows, we are bombarded with morning breath commercials on television. How do these commercials equate with what is happening in your own life and how did that person smell to you the day before, compared to the morning after?

Do you take your sense of hearing for granted? I am convinced that our younger generation is all going to suffer from some sort of hearing impairment by the time they are thirty. Their music is played at such an incredibly high decibel level that I don't see how the healthy ear can withstand that type of abuse over long periods of time. How do you listen to your music? And, in fact, what kind of music do you listen to?

Let's concentrate on music. Do you like one type of music and no other, or are your tastes more universal, or do you fall somewhere in between? It's not a bad idea to try and list the types of music that you like. My own tastes have formed from the classics to blues, jazz, classic rock, and new age. It all depends on the mood I am in. How do you feel about your music? Can you define your tastes? Can you take it one step further and also define the venues which you prefer to attend while listening to music?

What about other sounds? We are bombarded every day by white noise. If we work in an office we are surrounded by white noise from lights, air conditioning, computers, piped in music, telephones and innumerable variations on the theme. If it's possible, go to your work place when no one else is there. The profound sense of silence can almost hit you like the wall of white noise hits you on a daily basis. The difference is that we have become so attuned to the sound of white noise that we block it out. We are not attuned to the sounds of silence.

Do you listen to birds in the morning? Do you listen to arguments from your neighbours? Do you hear screeching tires? What are the sounds that have become familiar to you?

Take that piece of paper and pen and make a list of all the noises that you hear during the course of only one day, you will be absolutely astonished. You will be astonished at two things. The first is that so many of these noises did not make any type of conscious awareness for you. The second is, that you had no idea that so many noises existed in your daily life.

Many years ago, when I was first married, my grandmother had not yet sold the farm. My husband was a city boy. My grandmother asked us to come down to the farm to choose our wedding presents among the many treasures she had tucked away.

For two days, only the three of us were on the farm. My husband could not stand the silence. He couldn't sleep and grew very restless. I, on the other hand, found it very soothing. It had been what I had grown up with. My husband had never experienced silence before in his life.

What kind of category do you fall into?

What about your sense of sight? Are you curious about what you see around you, or do you take it for granted, or do you fall somewhere in between? Most of us, I think, fall somewhere in between. We have certain routes we take to go to work, certain places to like to shop, certain places we prefer to go. As we become more familiar with all of these we look at them on a daily basis but we fail to see anything.

How do you nurture your sense of sight? I think this is really worth thinking about. I am fortunate enough to live in one of the most beautiful cities in the world. Not only do we have the ocean on one side, we are partially surrounded by a ring of mountains. Winter and summer, it is always green. Even when the skies are gray, we can still see green. In fact, we are known for living in a rain forest.

Many people who have grown up here and who have spent their lives here do not always notice a great deal of the beauty that is always around them. They take it for granted. Those of us who have migrated here are always going through periods of being awestruck at the beauty around us.

Some people are awestruck at the beauty of the mountains in the winter. I am continually awestruck at the beauty and colours of the spring. When was the last time you looked around at your city or town? When was the last time you really saw it? We all look at things, but do we see them?

We are not going to balance all of our five senses. One or two of them are going to be more dominant than others. People in the field of Neurolinguistic programming have done some remarkable research on this. For example, if you are an auditory person, and you are with someone who is highly visual, each of you will relate to a situation in a different way. While one person is busy looking at something, the other is busy hearing what's going on around him.

Tie in all of the gifts of your sensuality. They are part of your persona. They are part of who you are. Let them bloom. You can only benefit.

Sensuality, like anything else in life, is truly a matter of degrees. We open our senses to the extent that we can handle them, according to our environment.

We open our true sexuality in exactly the same way. That is the magic phrase "true sexuality". That is not the sexuality that is portrayed in today's society. True sexuality is the type of sexuality that is healthy. It is within each of us to reach that healing place of sexuality. It takes work and it is worth it.

The more we become attuned to our senses and our sensuality, the more we can live at a higher level of consciousness, and it becomes easier to stay tuned in.

The reverse is also true. The more we shut down, the more baggage we carry around, the less aware we are of our sensuality. Because nature hates a vacuum, we will set up ways to feed that very basic need. Often the way we do that is with blatant sexuality. The blatant sexuality portrayed in pornography, in a great many movies, and even in people's graphic conversations with each other, in my opinion, lets me know that these people, through some circumstance, are shutting down.

Is that really what any of us wants? I don't think so. I think we all want and, indeed, crave a great deal more.

I don't believe we can have full and satisfying sexual experiences with our partners unless we are in tune with our senses and we are more in tune with our senses when we are in tune with ourselves.

I don't think it is possible to have good sex without good sensuality. The two simply don't correlate. I also don't think it's possible to have good sex until there is a meeting of the minds and a meeting of the heart. That doesn't mean that I have to agree with every thought and gesture that my partner has, but it does mean that I have to honour and respect him as an individual in his own right.

It doesn't necessarily follow that I have to love my partner in the conventional sense. Perhaps, all I need is a deep sense of caring. If that deep sense of caring and mutual respect is there, and it comes from the brain and the heart, the sensuality cannot help but flow between the two of us, and from that sensuality, sexuality will just happen.

Good sex, like everything else in life, needs to be learned. Everybody knows what various parts of the anatomy are for, but how to use them to the best advantage for ourselves and our partners is a whole other detail that a lot of people miss. But practice makes perfect, and that is where all the fun is.

That deep sense of fullness comes when each partner is not only committed to his or her own sense of well being, but to the sense of well being of his or her partner.

When that is achieved, then sex becomes a fulfilling pastime. Women who go from one conquest to another, I think, are looking for that sense of fulfillment. They never find it. It is very difficult to find that type of fulfillment in a game of bedroom gymnastics.

You may be physically relieved of physical tension you are carrying around but it is impossible to feel any emotional contact if you have not allowed your respective sensualities to intermingle.

In fact, sex used as a weapon can be a very strong deterrent to intimacy.

What is the best way of staying out of somebody's head? What is the best way of **not** getting to know them?

One of the best ways of staying out of someone's head and keeping your distance is by having a good roll in the hay and not spending any time getting to know each other.

I think it is a sad commentary on our times that people have chosen not to invest any of their time and energy into the magic of courtship.

If people were to spend more time on courtship, spend more quality time getting to know each other, and connected in their minds and their hearts first, I bet we would see a significant decline in the divorce rate. When people are willing to commit at this level you can be assured these people are comfortable within their own skins.

Besides, what have you got to lose? The alternative has been a divorce rate that is in excess of 50%. We have tens of thousands of unwanted pregnancies, women who are starving themselves in the name of fashion and sexuality, men who are looking for yet another notch on their belt. And lots of very dangerous STD's.

At this point in our evolution we are certainly in a lose/lose situation. By studying our sensuality issues we can reach our sexuality issues, open them up, take a look, see what's bothering us, and move on to the next step.

We are not going to do this in a week or two. Sometimes it takes years. But, if we fall over, we just pick ourselves up and start over. Because, frankly, we have no other choice. Not if we care about ourselves. And we do care. So we continue to work at it until we get it right. Right for us, right for our partner. That is when we know it has been worth it.

BEING CHILDISH or LOVING THE CHILD

When I first began listening to people talk about doing their inner child work, I had absolutely no idea where they were coming from.

It took me many, many months of reading and listening to other people's experiences and opinions before I was able to formulate what this all meant.

It finally came together through a workshop I was taking. This workshop was given through the Family Services Bureau and was based on the healing techniques that are given in Robin Norwood's book "Women who Love Too Much".

The workshop lasted for six weeks and was made up entirely of women of course, and was pretty intensive stuff.

Indeed, about 30% of the women involved found it to be a little too much to handle and dropped out. I can only hope that, at a later time, each of those women was able to continue on with this very important part of her healing work.

The Facilitator of this workshop asked us to spend a week, if necessary, writing a letter to the little girl that was in each of us. That was one of the toughest assignments I ever faced in my life. I didn't even know where to begin. The only thing I could do was to put myself in a meditative state, get my committee of assholes out of the way, and begin writing.

With your permission, I would like to share the letter I wrote to the little girl that lives inside of me:

> *"To my child within me,*
>
> *For a long time after I became an adult I didn't think of you in terms of ever being a child, or the child that lived within me. Uncle Wally has pictures, and when I looked at them, it was like looking at some little girl that grew up in a life I had very little recollection of and didn't want to face. You were a stranger. You stayed that way for many, many years. I used to look at your picture thinking you were a neglected kid, had no friends, and no family that cared, no-one to talk to. You were lonely. I still didn't associate that with me. That little girl became someone else – I wanted to get on with my life.*
>
> *Now, as the memories start coming back, bit by bit, I see you as someone vulnerable and scared, someone who still is struggling*

for answers. I see you as confused and at odds with the reality I have chosen for you — not much different than the child you were so long ago. I see you as someone crying for love and doing it in many ways. You're not the rebel you were a long time ago. It's almost as if I can feel your love for me, your protector and that you know I will still make mistakes, but I'm trying to make up to both of us, for all the hurt we suffered back then, and I have carried with us as an adult.

I love you. I don't want to see you hurt anymore. I want you to be happy and joyful. Caring and good. I love you for the trust you are starting to place in me. I carry you wherever I go and embrace and try and protect you when my adult self still falls into a path of hurt. I'm trying to teach you to forgive, you were surrounded by so much illness. I want you to feel protected and content, knowing that I will never hurt you intentionally.

If I keep my faith in God, surround myself with good people, stay in touch with my own feelings, carefully look after our bodily needs, then we can both be winners in life.

You are always with me now and I am grateful for that, because it means that I no longer feel that lonely — and neither do you.

When I do something foolish sometimes I don't bring you into my life because I don't want you hurt anymore, but I know, with a knowingness deep inside, that as long as we walk together, life will be better. We are a team, you and I, and we will always be one.

I love you deeply."

The letter that you have just read is the letter I wrote to my little girl, my inner child, on March 4, 1987. When I look at it now, there is not one word in it I would change. It is as true for me today as it was back then.

I came to realize that one of the ways we block access to our inner child is by continually doing our own dysfunctional dance. It's tough being real in our society. It's tough being real in the work place, in relationships. It's tough being real walking down the street, going shopping, applying for a job, going out on a date. Getting real isn't easy.

We set ourselves up in all sorts of ways. Because we have been trying to deal with our own personal invalidation for most of our lives we are continually looking for validation from those around us. Until we get in touch with our inner child, very often the only way we think we can find this validation is by setting ourselves up as our own puppets and pulling our own strings. If I pull this string on me here, you are going to reach over there. If I continue to pull that string, you will react this way. I am so busy watching for your reaction as I continue pulling the strings on my own puppet, that I forget who I am. I am so busy forgetting who I am that I am also forgetting who you are because I am only watching you react to me.

Another interesting thing about this analogy is that, of course, a puppeteer cannot pull his own puppet. It is physically impossible for each of us to be our own puppeteer. We just keep falling over. So, if we are having problems pulling our own "right strings" then maybe we can reach over and pull someone else's "right strings". Then we can get into our control issues, and then we are into another vicious cycle. And the whole thing, if it weren't so sick, borders on the ridiculous.

Besides, the more we pull strings, the more uptight we become. The more uptight we become the more we pull strings. The more we pull strings and uptight we become, the less we know about that little child deep inside each of us. Because we don't have time for that anymore. We are now continually running to the next "show". It's no wonder our society is in such a mess. If we are all so busy pulling our own strings to keep ourselves up, as we watch each other's actions, how in the world can we ever be real? It doesn't happen that way. We must let it go. And we must let it go by allowing ourselves to get in touch with our inner child.

That inner child that dwells within, very often was not validated as a youngster. That's why we keep acting out. Once we begin giving validation to that child within us, we begin to heal.

You cannot be with your inner child if you are carrying lots of baggage. Whatever persona you are carrying around will get in the way of touching your inner spirit. The only way you can reach that inner child is to be totally real.

There is a wonderful benefit to this. This is when we can come out and play on a healthy level. Most of us Adult Children lost the ability to play at a very early age. To learn to play now is such a wonderful bonus, that at times it can be overwhelming.

To achieve any of these benefits, we must continue to concentrate on the baggage we carry with us.

Accessing our inner child requires us to be totally removed from our baggage. And just "be".

When we get to that very special place in each of us that says we don't feel any compulsion to act out any developmental needs we can go to our own source and just "be".

And when we reach that special place, that is the true meaning of the word JOY.

Have you ever tried it?

Please do.

Find your pen and paper. Put yourself in a quiet and relaxed environment. Now, start a letter to you. That letter will now begin healing those deep seated wounds that only you know are there. Make that letter as short or as long as you need, and let it flow. The letter may be a paragraph. It may be twenty pages. It doesn't matter. You are going to you, in you, deep within you, to that little girl or boy who needs your love.

Write to him and tell him so. Tell him anything that you want, but most of all tell him that you love him.

Once you validate that inner child, you begin to validate yourself. When we validate ourselves, other people validate us, as well. Now we are into a happy circle A circle of recovery. It becomes easier to access the joy that each of us feels deep within. It becomes easier to access the pain each of us feels within. It becomes easier to access us.

Finally, we are getting to know who we really are. We don't have to act out our past traumas to try and prove anything to anyone. We are who we are. The relief is profound.

Try it. You will be amazed. And I promise you – you will never be sorry.

The Twelve Steps

Step 1

We admitted we were powerless and that our lives had become unmanageable.

Step 2

Came to believe that a Power greater than ourselves could restore us to sanity.

Step 3

Made a decision to turn our will and our lives over to the care of God <u>as we understand Him</u>.

Step 4

Made a searching and fearless moral inventory of ourselves.

Step 5

Admitted to God, to ourselves, and to another human being the exact nature of our wrongs.

Step 6

Were entirely ready to have God remove all these defects of character.

Step 7

Humbly asked God to remove our shortcomings.

Step 8

Made a list of all persons we had harmed, and became willing to make amends to them all.

Step 9

Made direct amends to such people, wherever possible, except when to do so would injure them or others.

Step 10

Continued to take personal inventory and when we were wrong promptly admitted it.

Step 11

Sought through prayer and meditation to improve our conscious contact with God <u>as we understand Him</u>, praying only for knowledge of His will for us and the power to carry that out.

Step 12

Having had a spiritual awakening as a result of theses steps, we tried to carry this message to others, and to practice these principals in all our affairs.

Printed in the United States
By Bookmasters